CW00924805

Ancient
Philosophy

A Beginner's Guide

3303255062

**ONEWORLD BEGINNER'S GUIDES** combine an original, inventive, and engaging approach with expert analysis on subjects ranging from art and history to religion and politics, and everything in-between. Innovative and affordable, books in the series are perfect for anyone curious about the way the world works and the big ideas of our time.

aesthetics
africa
american politics
anarchism
ancient philosophy
animal behaviour
anthropology
anti-capitalism
aquinas
archaeology
art
artificial intelligence
the baha'i faith
the beat generation
the bible
biodiversity
bioterror & biowarfare
the brain
british politics
the Buddha
cancer
censorship
christianity
civil liberties
classical music
climate change
cloning
the cold war
conservation
crimes against humanity
criminal psychology
critical thinking
the crusades
daoism
democracy
descartes
dewey
dyslexia
economics

energy
engineering
the english civil wars
the enlightenment
epistemology
ethics
the european union
evolution
evolutionary psychology
existentialism
fair trade
feminism
forensic science
french literature
the french revolution
genetics
global terrorism
hinduism
history
the history of medicine
history of science
homer
humanism
huxley
international relations
iran
islamic philosophy
the islamic veil
journalism
judaism
lacan
life in the universe
literary theory
machiavelli
mafia & organized crime
magic
marx
medieval philosophy
the middle east

modern slavery
NATO
the new testament
nietzsche
nineteenth-century art
the northern ireland conflict
nutrition
oil
opera
the palestine–israeli conflict
parapsychology
particle physics
paul
philosophy
philosophy of mind
philosophy of religion
philosophy of science
planet earth
postmodernism
psychology
quantum physics
the qur'an
racism
rawls
reductionism
religion
renaissance art
the roman empire
the russian revolution
shakespeare
shi'i islam
the small arms trade
sufism
the torah
the united nations
the victorians
volcanoes
the world trade organization
world war II

# Ancient Philosophy

## A Beginner's Guide

William J. Prior

ONEWORLD

A Oneworld Paperback Original

Published in North America, Great Britain and Australia by
Oneworld Publications, 2016

ISBN 978-1-78074-341-7
eISBN 978-1-78074-342-4

Typeset by Silicon Chips
Printed and bound in Great Britain
by Clays Ltd, St Ives plc

Oneworld Publications
10 Bloomsbury Street
London WC1B 3SR
England

# To Peg

# CONTENTS

# Contents

# Acknowledgments

I would like to thank the following individuals for their assistance: my research assistant, Byron Mongillo; my colleagues Brian Buckley, Scott LaBarge, and Erick Ramirez, who read chapters of an earlier version of the manuscript; an anonymous referee for the press, who read the penultimate version; and most especially Tom Blackson, who read the entire manuscript in the penultimate version. They saved me from many errors; I am of course responsible for those that remain. Thanks finally to the editors of Oneworld Publications, especially Mike Harpley, who guided this project from its inception to completion.

# Abbreviations

I use the following abbreviations to refer to ancient sources:

Aristotle:
| | |
|---|---|
| *De Anima* | *De An.* |
| *Metaphysics* | *Metaph.* |
| *Nicomachean Ethics* | *E. N.* |

Homer:
| | |
|---|---|
| *Odyssey* | *Od.* |

Plato:
| | |
|---|---|
| *Apology* | *Ap.* |
| *Euthyphro* | *Euthyphr.* |
| *Gorgias* | *Grg.* |
| *Phaedo* | *Phd.* |
| *Republic* | *R.* |
| *Symposium* | *Smp.* |
| *Theaetetus* | *Tht.* |
| *Timaeus* | *Ti.* |

Xenophon:
| | |
|---|---|
| *Memorabilia* | *Mem.* |

fragment (a quotation from a Sophist or Presocratic philosopher):     fr.

# Introduction

In 399 BCE, a shabbily dressed, unattractive, eccentric old man named Socrates was put on trial in the Greek city-state of Athens for impiety and corrupting the youth. His accusers said he did not believe in the gods the city honored but introduced strange new divinities. The latter charge probably refers to the fact that Socrates claimed that a divine voice spoke to him on occasions when he was about to do something wrong, forbidding him to do it. He was convicted; his accusers demanded, and got, the death penalty. Socrates died by drinking a poison made from the hemlock plant.

## SOCRATES

Socrates was a citizen of Athens, born about 469 BCE. In a culture devoted to beauty, Socrates stood out for being physically unattractive, with a snub nose and bulging eyes. Perhaps the best account of Socrates we have comes from one of his companions, Alcibiades, in a speech in Plato's *Symposium*; Alcibiades says that Socrates went into trances: on one occasion he remained motionless, lost in thought, for a day and a night. When he served in the Athenian army during Athens' great war with Sparta (the Peloponnesian War, 431–404), he behaved heroically in combat. All in all, Alcibiades says, there was no one like him. It is for his intellectual prowess, however, that Socrates is best remembered. He claimed that he had no knowledge of "the greatest matters": chiefly the question that most interested him, how we ought to live, but he was a fearsome critic of everyone he encountered who thought they did know about such things, including the leading public figures of the day. He tried to show his fellow citizens that they were devoting themselves to the wrong things, such as power and wealth, when what they should be caring about was the state of their souls.

Socrates was a public figure in Athens. He conducted his examinations of people in many places, but often in the city's marketplace. Comic playwrights wrote plays about him, one of which, Aristophanes' *Clouds*, we still possess. In part because of his celebrity, he acquired a bad reputation among many Athenians. Some hated him so much (perhaps because he had humiliated them in public) that they had him tried, convicted, and executed. Though Socrates inspired hatred, he also inspired fierce devotion. He denied being a teacher, but he had many followers, often young people, who imitated his method of argument. Socrates himself wrote nothing, but some of his followers created a new literary genre, the "Socratic conversation," portraying Socrates in conversation with others. Two of them, Plato and Xenophon, wrote works about him that can be read today.

You might expect that this trial and execution, like so many others from the distant past, would long ago have been forgotten. Yet Socrates is probably the best-known philosopher, and in fact the most famous person from ancient Greek civilization, in the world today. Why is this so? Why is Socrates the "face" of ancient philosophy? Why is he philosophy's hero, its martyr, its saint? What did Socrates do that so angered his enemies that they wanted to see him dead, or at least exiled from Athens? Why did his disciples admire him so much that they wrote literary works designed to preserve his memory, to explain to people who he was?

One of these works, Plato's *Apology of Socrates*, offers an answer to these questions. It purports to be the defense speech Socrates gave at his trial. It remains today one of the most widely read classics of philosophy. Plato saw Socrates as the innocent victim of an unjust prosecution, carried out by angry men who utterly failed to understand who he was. Who was he? In probably the most famous image of the *Apology*, Socrates says that he is a gadfly, given to Athens by the god Apollo, to stir it up, to make the Athenians stop thinking primarily about pleasure, wealth, and power, and start thinking about the state of their souls. He wanted them to ask themselves how they ought to live. He did not want to *tell* them how to live, only to get them to think about the question for themselves. In another famous passage, he said that the unexamined life, the life without inquiry, is not worth living for a human being. Socrates was tried and convicted because he wanted to turn the people of Athens from a life that took for granted the values of their society to one in which they questioned those values and sought a more rational basis for their lives.

This devotion to a life of inquiry is what made Socrates seem a threat to some Athenians and a model worth following to others. There were doubtless other reasons for his trial and conviction. Socrates challenged the moral authority of the political leaders of Athens, and this angered them. He did it, moreover, with great personal charisma. Socrates was far from alone among critics of traditional values in Athens. He was part of an intellectual revolution that took place in the last half of the fifth century. He stood out, and he continues to stand out, among the group of intellectuals who were part of that revolution, in part because of the powerful personal effect he had on people. As Alcibiades put it:

> I have heard Pericles and many other great orators, and I have admired their speeches. But nothing like this ever happened to me: they never upset me so deeply that my very own soul started protesting that my life—*my* life!—was no better than the most miserable slave's.
>
> (Plato, *Smp.* 215e)

Socrates' challenge to popular culture and moral practice could not be ignored, in part, because Socrates could not be ignored. In Socrates, philosophy had a public presence philosophy has not had since. He was a popular icon; in modern terms, a celebrity.

A life of inquiry is difficult; as the American philosopher William James put it, "a great many people think they are thinking when they are really just rearranging their prejudices." Socrates left behind no answer to his basic question, apart from saying that we ought to devote our lives to self-examination, to inquiry. He made it impossible for some people to accept the values they had inherited from their culture, but the only ideal he substituted for those values was the life of the philosopher, the seeker after wisdom. For that is what philosophy is, at its root: a life of inquiry into the most basic questions one can ask, a search for understanding. Socrates, we might say, created a vacuum with his question. Other philosophers quickly rushed in to fill that vacuum. They, along with Socrates, are the subject of this book.

I offer here an introduction to ancient philosophy by way of the person of Socrates and the questions he raised or led others to raise. There are other ways to present ancient philosophy. Socrates was not the first philosopher: for over a century and a half before him, other philosophers, whom we know as the "Presocratics," had investigated the world of nature.

## THE PRESOCRATICS

"Presocratic" philosophy is so named because most of the philosophers referred to by the term lived before Socrates. (The last Presocratic, Democritus, was actually a younger contemporary of Socrates: he was born in about 460 and died about 370.) A better name for the group might be Aristotle's: he called them the "physical philosophers." They were concerned with discovering the first principle of nature. The earliest philosophers, beginning with Thales of Miletus (c. 625–c. 546), focused on matter, usually one of the "four elements"—earth, water, air, or fire—as the first principle. They thought of the primary element as being naturally active, producing the other elements and, eventually, the entire world-order. Some Presocratics sought for a first principle other than the elements; Xenophanes (c. 570–c. 475) called his first principle "God"; Anaxagoras (c. 510–428) referred to his as "Mind." The followers of Pythagoras (c. 570–c. 495) thought that the first principles of nature were numbers.

Three of the most important Presocratic philosophers are Heraclitus (c. 535–c. 475), Parmenides (c. 515–c. 460), and Democritus. Heraclitus was an enigmatic writer; the ancients saw him as positing a world of constant change, a world in which nothing remains the same from moment to moment. His symbol of change was fire, which he associated with God. Modern interpreters have seen in Heraclitus, in contrast, a proponent of a unifying principle, which he called the *logos* (literally, "word," but probably something like "reason" for Heraclitus), which made change intelligible. Parmenides, however, challenged the intelligibility of change. Change, he argued, involved "not-being" (as we might say today, in change a state of affairs comes to be that did not exist previously) but "not-being" does not exist. "Not-being," according to Parmenides, was nothing, and nothing can come from nothing. So change is impossible. The cosmos, said Parmenides, had to be a single unchanging whole, limited on all sides, "like a well-rounded sphere." This argument troubled all of Parmenides' successors, who tried to retain his idea that nothing can come to be from nothing, but also defend the reality of change in the universe. Perhaps the boldest response to Parmenides' challenge was that of the atomists, Democritus and Leucippus, who declared that "not-being," by which they meant empty space, existed just as much as being, by which they meant an infinite number of indivisible, imperceptible particles—atoms.

The Presocratics asked a basic question about that world: what is its ruling principle, its ultimate cause? They asked about the relation between the world we experience and the ultimate reality on which it is based, a question that is the basis of modern science. They offered a variety of answers to this question, at least one of which, the atomic theory, is the direct ancestor of contemporary particle physics. Their question did not concern Socrates, but it certainly concerned his followers. I don't say much in this book about the Presocratics; I speak of them only incidentally. Despite the fact that ancient philosophy begins with them, I do not think that their question provides the best introduction, the best "way in," to ancient philosophy. In my opinion, it is Socrates' question that does that. If you want to plunge into the subject of ancient philosophy, if you want to immerse yourself in it, it is with Socrates that you should start. As the Roman orator and philosophical writer Cicero (106–43) said in his *Tusculan Disputations*, V. 10, "Socrates was the first to call philosophy down from the heavens and to place it in cities, and even to introduce it into homes and compel it to inquire about life and standards and goods and evils." Socrates was right to do so. Philosophical inquiry must begin with the fundamental question we face as human beings, the question how we ought to live. Other questions can, and inevitably will, come later.

My approach in this book is therefore not strictly chronological. I don't begin, as many introductions do, with the Presocratics. I begin with the "second beginning" of philosophy, the one that occurred when Socrates called philosophy down from the heavens and placed it in our cities and homes. I discuss first the question that most concerned Socrates, and I look at several answers that were proposed by his successors: Plato, Aristotle, the Stoics, the Epicureans, and the ancient Skeptics. Socrates' question led to others. Socrates suggests in the *Apology* that the height of human knowledge might be the recognition of the extent of our ignorance. Yet he also insists that we ought to seek to live virtuously, and suggests that virtue is knowledge of a very high order: knowledge of good and evil. But what is knowledge? Can we attain knowledge of what Socrates called "the greatest matters?" Moreover, Socrates said that we ought to put care of our souls above all other concerns: but what is the soul? Does it even exist? And, if it does, how is it related to the body? Is it immortal, or does it cease to exist when we die? Finally, I discuss the question that led to the official charges against Socrates, that of the existence of the gods. Do the gods exist? If so, what is their nature? Do they interact with us? If so, is that interaction for our benefit, or is it harmful? Should we fear the gods, or should we aspire to the kind of existence they have? The gods of ancient Greek mythology are dead, but the questions whether there is a God, and whether this God is concerned with our welfare are still alive. So, I believe, are all of the questions I have raised above. Socrates is a historical figure, a citizen of Athens who lived in the latter half of the fifth century in a civilization in some respects very different from our own, but he is also as contemporary as any philosopher living today. So are the ancient philosophical debates that he started or substantially changed by his life of inquiry.

This book is an introduction to ancient philosophy, as the title says, a beginner's guide. I don't presuppose any familiarity with the ancient philosophers I discuss, but I hope what I have written will lead you to read the classic texts of ancient philosophy and confront the philosophers I discuss first hand. It is these classic texts—Plato's dialogues, Aristotle's treatises, Cicero's dialogues, Lucretius' Latin epic poem *On the Nature of Things*, the letters and essays of Seneca, the *Discourses* and *Handbook* of Epictetus, the *Meditations* of Marcus Aurelius, and the skeptical writings of Sextus Empiricus—that formed the basis of a conversation about the nature of philosophy that has been fundamental down to the present day. They are basic to an understanding of the Western intellectual tradition. For a time in the Middle Ages, most of these works were lost in the West, though they were studied in the Muslim world. When they were rediscovered—first the writings of Aristotle, but then Plato's dialogues and the works of Cicero and others—they sparked an intellectual revolution that was unprecedented. To study the Renaissance, in particular, is to see the profound effect the recovery of these works had on people at the time. They still affect people who read them in the same way. These classic works offer readers perspectives on the nature of life and how to live it, the nature of knowledge and reality, the nature of the soul and its relation to the body, and the nature of the place of human beings in the universe, that are still relevant today. They remain, I believe, the best introduction to what philosophy is about. My aim in this book is simply to whet your appetite for these works, to explain why you should make them your point of entry for the study of philosophy.

# 1
# The good life

*As long as I draw breath and am able, I shall not cease to practice philosophy, to exhort you and in my usual way to point out to any one of you whom I happen to meet: Good Sir, you are an Athenian, a citizen of the greatest city with the greatest reputation for both wisdom and power; are you not ashamed of your eagerness to possess as much wealth, reputation and honors as possible, while you do not care for nor give thought to wisdom or truth, or the best possible state of your soul?*

(Plato's *Apology*)

## Athens   background

Athens in the last half of the fifth century BCE *was* a great city, admired for both its wisdom and its power. Twice in the first half of the century she had defeated, against long odds, an invading force from the vast Persian Empire (whose emperor was known simply as "the Great King"), and led, with Sparta, a coalition that expelled the Persians from Greece for good. She was the prime mover in an alliance of Greek city-states organized to make sure the Persians did not return. She was the leading democracy in Greece, the inventor of the idea of democratic government.

Her tragic and comic playwrights were the envy of the Greek-speaking world. Her greatest political leader, Pericles, was constructing on the high ground of the city known as the Acropolis a set of monumental buildings, including the Parthenon, to which visitors still flock today. These were heady times—great days to be an Athenian. And new ideas were circulating in the intellectual atmosphere of Athens, ideas brought to the city by philosophers of two distinct sorts—the philosophers of nature we refer to as the "Presocratics," and the itinerant teachers of ethics, political theory, and rhetoric we call the "Sophists"—who were drawn to Athens because of her wealth and power. These two groups challenged the traditional ideas and values that had shaped Athenian culture for centuries. They brought about an intellectual revolution. Looking back from the vantage point of later centuries, it has seemed to many that this was a "golden age," an age of enlightenment.

By the beginning of the fourth century, however, Athens was in eclipse, her wealth and dominant power a thing of the past. She had lost a long and destructive war with Sparta—her one-time ally in the war against the Persians—fought from 431 to 404 over the question of the political supremacy of Greece. The intoxicating ideas that had sparked the intellectual revolution of the fifth century, ideas that had undermined the traditional culture, seemed now to many people to have been less like wine than vinegar.

## Socrates

Through this period of political and intellectual ferment lived Socrates. According to Plato's *Apology*, Socrates had no interest in the philosophy of nature. He was, however, interested in the questions of ethics and politics that had engaged the Sophists, and in his dialogues Plato shows us Socrates in conversation with them and with their disciples, as well as with ordinary Athenians.

## PLATO

Plato was an Athenian citizen, probably born in the mid-420s. He was from an aristocratic family. As a young man, he considered a life in politics; he was invited to become an associate of the tyranny of "the Thirty," an autocratic government imposed on Athens by Sparta after Athens' defeat in the Peloponnesian War. (Plato's uncle Critias was a leading member of the Thirty.) The unjust conduct of this regime appalled Plato, however, and he steered clear of it. When the Thirty were overthrown and democracy restored, he thought again of a political life, but the trial and conviction of Socrates convinced him that only the rule of philosophers could bring an end to corruption in government. (So says the *Seventh Platonic Letter*, which may or may not have been written by Plato, but which was at least very probably written by someone close enough to Plato to have knowledge of events in his life.) He never gave up on the attempt to found a government led by a philosopher: he made three trips to Sicily, in 388, 367, and 361, in an unsuccessful attempt to convert the rulers of Syracuse to philosophy.

If Plato was a failure at practical politics, he was just the opposite as a philosopher. He had been, probably for the last decade of Socrates' life, one of his closest companions. Like other companions of Socrates, he wrote "Socratic conversations," dialogues. These dialogues combine Plato's own reflections on Socrates with original philosophical argument, in such a way that it is difficult to tell what is Socratic reminiscence and what Platonic creation. These dialogues, as well as being recognized as among the greatest works in the history of philosophy, are among the finest prose works written in ancient Greek. Homer and Plato are the only ancient authors all of whose works have come down to us intact. At some point in his life, probably in the mid-380s, he founded the Academy, the first institution of higher education in the Western world, near a grove of olive trees sacred to the goddess Athena, about a mile outside Athens. He attracted to it several of the greatest minds of his generation, original researchers in astronomy and mathematics as well as philosophy. Among those who entered the Academy was Aristotle, who was a member there from 367 to Plato's death in 347. Plato made fundamental contributions to philosophy in many areas, from ethics and political philosophy to metaphysics, epistemology, philosophical psychology, the philosophy of nature, philosophical theology, and aesthetics. His works are still studied today.

Socrates, as I stated in the Introduction, was the "public face" of the intellectual revolution. He examined public figures, including the leading political leaders of the day. He made a lot of enemies. Now the Athenians prized, and celebrated, free speech. They thought that they were the freest city in Greece. But some of those enemies he had created decided that there were limits to free speech, and that Socrates' constant criticism was a luxury they could not afford, especially in the aftermath of the city's humiliating defeat and the subsequent tyranny of "the Thirty," the oligarchic government that ruled Athens in a "reign of terror" in 404–3, So they had him put on trial, and the outcome was that he was convicted and executed.

Many explanations have been given for Socrates' trial, conviction, and execution. It is unlikely that he would have been tried at all if Athens had not lost the Peloponnesian War. In Plato's *Apology*, Socrates blamed his "first accusers," such as the comic playwright Aristophanes, who spread rumors that he was both a philosopher of nature (which he denied) and a Sophist, who must as a result be an atheist and corruptor of youth. Some interpreters, discounting the religious nature of the charges against Socrates, have sought an explanation for his trial in his associations with Critias, ringleader of the Thirty, and Alcibiades, a controversial Athenian leader who went over to the Spartan side during the Peloponnesian War for a while, before later switching back to the Athenians. There is probably some truth in each of the explanations that have been offered. As to his conviction once he had been put on trial, Plato's *Apology* gives us plenty of reasons for that. Socrates claimed that the Oracle of Delphi, the most revered source of prophecy in ancient Greece, had declared that no one was wiser than he. He compared himself to Achilles, the greatest of the heroes of Homer's *Iliad*. He said that he was the god's gift to Athens, a gadfly sent by Apollo to stir the city from its slumbers. He refused to placate the jurors by an appeal to pity. When he was asked to propose an alternative to the death penalty asked for by his accusers, he initially proposed that he be given free meals at the city's expense, a privilege reserved for Olympic victors. All of this would no doubt have sounded like arrogance to the jurors, who were used to defendants begging for mercy.

Socrates was the victim of a public reaction to the intellectual revolution he helped to create. The conflict in values that arose in the fifth century was between two views I'll call "traditionalism" and "modernism." Traditionalism was simply the adherence to the inherited cultural beliefs and practices of the past. It was not a particularly reflective view; it was based on the claim that "we've always done things this way." Traditionalists assumed that their beliefs were true, that the values they upheld were objective, that the Athenian way of doing things was the right way. They appealed to the gods as the source of those values, and they appealed to the poets, and especially Homer, "the educator of Greece," in support of their tradition. But Homer's epic works, the *Iliad* and *Odyssey*, were actually composed centuries earlier and described a civilization that existed centuries before that, if it had actually existed at all. The fact was that the values, traditions, customs, and laws of Athens differed from those of twelfth-century Homeric society, and from the values of the cities and countries the Athenians encountered in the fifth century. How could the same gods justify one ethical framework in Athens and another in Sparta, or in Persia?

Traditionalism was stretched to the breaking point by modernism, which *was* a reflective point of view. Modernism was the view of a small number of thinkers, mainly the Sophists, who offered their own ideas of value as more enlightened than the traditional views. The most famous of this group, Protagoras, attempted to do away with traditionalism with two brief remarks: "Man is the measure of all things: of the things that are that they are, and of the things that are not that they are not" (fragment 1); and "Concerning the gods I am unable to discover whether they exist or not, or what they are like in form; for there are many hindrances to knowledge, the obscurity of the subject and the brevity of human life" (fr. 4). If by "man" Protagoras meant the individual and not humankind in general, then so much for tradition; for who but I can decide what is right for me? Protagoras was a relativist. Moral absolutes did not exist for him, only the judgments of people, which differed from city to city and even from person to person. Protagoras was a cultural conservative, however: he thought one ought to obey the customs of the city one lived in. He was a practical traditionalist, if not a theoretical one. But he opened the door to a more extreme version of modernism that we see not only in Plato's dialogues, but in other Athenian writers as well. For if tradition and culture are swept away, and the gods as well, what is left as the basis of action, of the conduct of life, other than the pursuit of pleasure and power? Plato shows us two characters advocating just such views: the Sophist Thrasymachus in Book I of the *Republic* and the politician Callicles in the *Gorgias*. He does not portray them as attractive people.

Socrates was no friend of tradition. He dismissed the study of poetry, the basic means of traditional education, as something akin to "second-rate drinking parties," of people who bring in flute players for entertainment because they can't conduct a worthwhile discussion themselves. He demanded a rational justification for people's conduct, and traditionalism was short on that. Time and time again, Socrates' conversations with ordinary Athenians, as described in Plato's dialogues, revealed that they could not explain or justify rationally their conduct, their way of life. He was no friend of the Sophists either, however, though he was often confused with them in the minds of those who did not know him well. Like the Sophists, Socrates was an intellectual, and he thought that the problems of ethics and politics should be solved by rational argument. But he thought that rhetoric, the art of public speaking that several of the Sophists taught, was basically a fraud: it persuaded people, but it left them ignorant.

He compared it to pastry baking, whose "goods" were tempting but unhealthy. He rejected the relativism of Protagoras; he sought rational knowledge of ethical terms that could be expressed in definitions that were universal, applicable to everyone. He did not think that "man" was the measure of things, but rather the wise man. He thought that wisdom was a kind of expert knowledge of the good, akin to the art of medicine or other forms of expertise. He rejected Protagoras' idea that wisdom was something that was possessed by everyone, and that could be taught "by all to all," like the Greek language. Because of this view of political wisdom, he was a critic of democracy as the Athenians practiced it. He criticized the Athenian practice of choosing people for political office by lot. He thought that government ought to be in the hands of the wise. Unlike Sophists such as Thrasymachus, who advocated a moral and political "realism" that treated the practice of traditional virtues such as justice as a "mug's game," Socrates regarded the virtues—wisdom, justice, temperance, courage, and piety—as the foundation of the good life. Socrates was revolutionary in demanding a rational account of the virtues, and in identifying all of them with wisdom, but he did not at all reject or condemn the life devoted to virtue. Quite the opposite. In this respect, he was more akin to traditionalists than to the Sophists, especially the more radical ones.

Socrates was a lightning rod for criticism both from Athenian traditionalists and from other intellectuals. It was the criticism of the traditionalists that in the end did him in. He could say, sincerely, that he believed in the gods (though the way he conceived of the gods, as perfect models of wisdom and thus of goodness, was very different from traditional mythology), but he could not deny that he was a critic of Athenian culture and politics. He could deny, sincerely, that he had any "teaching" to pass on to others, but he could not deny that the young people who followed him about and imitated his practice of examining others picked up his radical ideas about rational inquiry, the

virtues, the good life, and the gods. No wonder that Socrates
acquired enemies who saw him as a threat to the civic order (and
in ancient Greece honoring the gods of the city was a basic part
of promoting civic order, a matter of good citizenship) as well as
followers who were passionate in their devotion to him, and who
saw his method of inquiry as essential to the good life. Alcibiades,
who was quoted in the Introduction, says in the same speech that:

> if you were to listen to his arguments, at first they'd strike
> you as totally ridiculous ... He's always going on about
> pack asses, or blacksmiths, or cobblers, or tanners; he's
> always making the same tired old points in the same tired
> old words. If you are foolish, or simply unfamiliar with
> him, you'd find it impossible not to laugh at his arguments.
> But if you ... go beneath their surface, you'll realize that
> no other arguments make any sense. They're truly worthy
> of a god, bursting with figures of virtue inside. They're of
> great—no, of the greatest—importance for anyone who
> wants to become a fine and good man.
>
> (*Smp.* 221e–222a, substituting "fine and good"
> for "truly good")

(The Greek phrase I translate "fine and good" is *kalos k'agathos*,
and it is a commonly used one. It represents a cultural ideal, of
beauty, primarily but not simply physical beauty, combined with
goodness: a kind of overall excellence, nobility of character.) There
were only four possible responses to Socrates: you could ignore
him, not go near him; you could flee, once he had "bitten you
like a snake," which was Alcibiades' response; you could become a
follower, like several Athenians, but most especially Plato; or you
could hate and fear him so much you tried to silence him.

Who was this man, this philosopher, who elicited such
passionate responses from those he examined? As the great scholar
Gregory Vlastos put it, he was a man who was "all paradox."

He had a completely negative method of argument, called the elenchus (which simply means "test" or "examination"). Socrates asked questions, such as: "What is courage?" "What is temperance?" "What is justice?" "What is piety?" "What is virtue?" "What is beauty?" "What is friendship?" The people he asked always responded confidently, as if answering the question was the easiest thing in the world. Didn't everyone know what these terms meant? They would offer a definition of the term. Then Socrates would ask a number of additional questions, which seemed to have equally obvious answers. When his interlocutors (the people he is portrayed as conversing with in Plato's dialogues) had answered these, Socrates would then point out that their answers contradicted the original definition. It would seem that the interlocutor could reject either the original definition or the subsequent answers, but invariably he rejects the definition. Then the process repeats—another suggested definition, another series of questions, another negative conclusion—until the interlocutor finally admits that he does not know what the term in question means at all. At that point the examination ends. The interlocutor is perplexed where he has previously been confident; he is chastened, humbled. With arguments like this, Socrates virtually eviscerated the traditionalist picture of virtue. And he did the same to his modernist intellectual colleagues, the Sophists.

What Socrates' interlocutors do not grasp, or only dimly grasp, is that Socrates is searching for a different *kind* of answer than they are used to giving. They are used to thinking concretely, in terms of examples; Socrates asks them to think abstractly, in terms of one concept that fits all examples. They are unfamiliar with this type of thought and, not surprisingly, they are not good at it. Examples of this misunderstanding abound in Plato's dialogues. Euthyphro, seeking to define holiness, says it is the sort of thing he is doing, prosecuting the wrongdoer. Laches, a general, when asked to define courage, says that it is standing one's ground in battle. Meno, attempting to define virtue, enumerates several kinds of virtue: the virtue of a man, a woman, a child, and so on. Hippias, asked to define beauty, first says that it is a beautiful maiden, then gold. Socrates does not like any of these definitions, because they do not express the *essential nature* of the concept. He wants his interlocutors to think *conceptually* about the definitions of these terms. Socrates is not the inventor of abstract, conceptual thought; he has predecessors among the Presocratics. But Socrates is unique in the way he pounds home his point about what he wants. He decisively changes the focus of inquiry, making it philosophical, and this change—from the concrete modes of thought with which his interlocutors are at home to abstract, conceptual thought—is Socrates' greatest contribution to philosophy. The ability to think abstractly will from now on define the philosopher and separate him or her from ordinary people.

One wonders whether anything was left after this demolition project had taken place. No wonder that some Athenians saw in Socrates a dire threat to their culture. And yet ... at the very same time, Alcibiades tells us, these arguments are the only ones that make sense, and they are essential to anyone who wants to be a "fine and good man." What people who became disciples of Socrates saw in him was not merely a destructive critic, but a model of and guide to the good life. How is it possible that these two aspects of Socrates can coexist in the same person? That is part of the paradox of Socrates.

We don't often see Socrates ask, "What is the best life for a human being to live?" though it is the central question of two Platonic dialogues, the *Gorgias* and the *Republic*, but it is the question that lies behind his questions about the virtues. In the *Gorgias*, he argues that the life of virtue, specifically the virtue of justice, is superior to the life of pleasure. What did Socrates mean by "the good life?" When we hear the phrase, it is most often the life of pleasure that we think of, but perhaps also the life of freedom, wealth and power. "The good life" is a translation of the Greek word *eudaimonia*, which is usually translated "happiness";

but "happiness" in English normally denotes a rather subjective pleasant feeling, one that comes and goes, one that we have when our desires are satisfied. If that is what "happiness" means, it would be hard to deny that the happiest life would be the most pleasant, the one that had the greatest preponderance of happy feelings over painful ones. *Eudaimonia*, on the other hand, is more objective. It doesn't exclude pleasure, but it refers to something more stable and admirable; it presents an ideal. Some translators suggest "human flourishing," but this is a term of art, a philosophical construct, rather than a phrase of ordinary English. So I prefer "the good life" instead. The goal of Socrates was to explain what the good life was, and why those who practiced the virtues lived better lives than those who did not. Socrates' goal became the goal of all of the other philosophers whose views we shall consider in this chapter. Whatever answer they gave, they thought Socrates asked the right question. Every philosopher whose views we shall examine thought that the aim of ethics was the attainment of the good life. They are all, to use a current term, "eudaimonists"; the common outlook they present is "eudaimonism."

Socrates argues in the *Gorgias* that the best life for a human being is the life of justice, and in general of virtue. His argument, not just in the *Gorgias* but in other Platonic dialogues such as the *Crito*, is that wrongdoing damages one's soul. Wrongdoing is produced by vice; virtue produces only good actions. The good life is precisely the life in which one puts care of one's soul above all other goods. Socrates' challenge to the Athenians, the "Socratic gospel," is that they should do exactly that.

What is the effect of this Socratic approach to philosophy on his interlocutors? It varies, but one very common effect, in addition to perplexity, is a sense of frustration. Sometimes they direct their frustration at themselves, but often they direct it at Socrates. This frustration could take the form of anger. Thrasymachus accuses Socrates of being ironic, intentionally deceitful, in his refusal to state what justice is. Alcibiades generalizes

Thrasymachus' point in the *Symposium* when he says that Socrates' whole life is "a game of irony." Meno compares Socrates to a sorcerer and advises him not to leave Athens, for his own good. What is the source of this anger? Socrates' interlocutors think that they know the answer to his questions—as I have said above, they think the answers are obvious. Yet, when they state their answers, Socrates ties them in knots. They have the sense that Socrates is playing a series of verbal tricks on them, such as the Sophists were known for, and they don't like it. They feel as though Socrates must know the answer to his questions, and could perfectly well state it if he wanted to. They think the perplexity in which the Socratic dialogues end is a kind of wreck that is intentionally designed by Socrates to make fools of them.

Socrates, however, denies that he knows the answers. Sometimes, as at the beginning of the *Meno*, he indicates that his ignorance of the nature of virtue is complete; and if he does not know what virtue is, how can he answer Meno's question, can virtue be taught? But can Socrates be *completely* ignorant of the nature of virtue? After all, he has spent his entire life examining others about virtue; surely, one suspects, he has learned *something*, if only about what virtue is *not*, what definitions of virtue must fail. It is for this reason that his interlocutors think his professions of ignorance must be *ironic*. Does Socrates make these professions of ignorance with the intent to deceive his interlocutors, to lure them into elenctic argument, where he can refute them? Does he perhaps possess some kind of mental state that is not as strong as knowledge but stronger than ignorance? Socrates in the *Gorgias* says that his arguments are "of iron and adamant" and that anyone who disagrees with him is made to appear ridiculous; and yet, he says, "I do not know how these things are." At the end of the *Meno*, Socrates develops a distinction between knowledge and true belief; is it possible that Socrates may possess true belief, if he does not possess knowledge? Still, Socrates' professions of ignorance, particularly in the *Meno*, are very strong. One might think

that if Socrates had something like true belief he might at least
mention that fact, but he does not; he insists on his ignorance.
This is another part of the paradox of Socrates.

From what I have said so far about Socrates, he seems to be
a totally negative philosopher, an ignorant inquirer, one who
is utterly without answers to the questions he asks and whose
method of inquiry can only refute answers given by others. His
only answer to the question "What is the good life?" would be the
life of inquiry, the examined life; the life spent in search for the
answer to the question "What is the good life?" How could this
purely destructive critic have been an inspiration to people like
Alcibiades? How could he have acquired associates such as Plato,
who had, as we shall see, no shortage of answers to Socrates' questions? One answer to this question is that Socrates *had* answers—
a positive philosophy, or at least the outlines of one—despite
his profession of ignorance. Despite the negative features of the
Socratic dialogues, there are indications in them that Socrates may
have had some constructive views of his own.

First of all, Socrates thought that everyone desired the good
life—not what he or she *thought* was the good life, but what was
*really* the good life. If you could convince someone that the life he
or she was pursuing was not really good, then Socrates thought
that person would abandon that pursuit. Second, as I have noted,
Socrates saw virtue as the key to the good life. (In this, he sided with
traditionalism as against the more extreme versions of modernism,
which would reject the traditional virtues in favor of other qualities, such as ruthlessness and guile.) Third, he thought that there
was one rational account of virtue that applied to everyone. Whatever virtue is, it must be the same in a man or a woman, a child
or an old person, a free person or a slave. Fourth, he thought that
all the virtues were in some sense one: justice, temperance, courage, piety, and wisdom were so related that if you had one of them
you had them all. Fifth, he thought that what unified the virtues
was knowledge, a term he used interchangeably with wisdom.

Sixth, he thought that the basis of knowledge about any virtue was knowledge of its correct definition. He frequently said that he could not know any of the properties of a subject under investigation, or even identify instances of the term in question, if he didn't know *what* that thing was. (There must be more to knowledge than a definition of the term in question, however difficult that may be to attain. Knowledge must be sufficient to tell the person who has it what to do in specific situations. Since none of Socrates' interlocutors ever comes up with a successful definition, we are left guessing about how one would get from a general definition to knowledge of the best course of action in a particular case.)

Socrates' idea that virtue is knowledge (specifically, knowledge of good and evil) is itself paradoxical. We ordinarily think that more than knowledge is required for virtue: e.g. strength of will or well-trained inclinations. Socrates says in the *Protagoras*, however, that knowledge is not the kind of thing to be pushed around by other psychological properties, such as unruly inclinations. No, if someone knows what action will lead one to the good life, then one will do it. This paradox is connected to two others: first, the view that wrongdoing is (results from) ignorance, and, second, the view that moral weakness is impossible. If knowledge is all one needs to explain virtuous action, if it is sufficient in itself to bring virtuous action about, then it follows that all non-virtuous action results from the lack of knowledge, namely ignorance. If knowledge infallibly causes one to act virtuously, and thus well, then it is not possible for someone to know what is the virtuous thing to do and act against that knowledge. These three propositions—that virtue is knowledge, that wrongdoing is due to ignorance, and that moral weakness is impossible—are known as the "Socratic paradoxes." Socrates' view is commonly described as "intellectualist" because it appeals only to cognitive states such as knowledge and ignorance to explain right and wrong action, virtue and vice.

Did Socrates really believe in this intellectualist account of virtue? He never quite says to some interlocutor, "Here is my account of the matter; this is what I believe." Rather, he presents it as an account to be accepted or rejected by the interlocutor. In the *Meno*, he gets Meno to accept it, but then suggests that virtue is not to be defined as knowledge after all, but as either knowledge or right opinion. In the *Protagoras*, he presents the paradoxes as part of a hedonistic theory of the good, one that holds that the good is pleasure. Nowhere else in the dialogues does Socrates endorse such a view. In the *Republic*, Socrates puts forward a complex account of the virtues that allows for moral weakness, but most interpreters believe that in the *Republic* "Socrates," the character in the dialogue, is speaking for Plato. On the other hand, Aristotle presents the intellectualist account of virtue, vice, and moral weakness as Socrates' in his *Nicomachean Ethics*, and the Stoics adopt an intellectualist account of virtue that is indebted to the account attributed to Socrates in Plato's *Protagoras* and *Meno*.

Socrates thought that philosophy was care of the soul. Not only that, but he said that he constantly exhorted his fellow citizens to stop putting other so-called "goods," such as wealth, reputation, or honors, ahead of the pursuit of wisdom and truth. He himself pursued wisdom with a single-minded determination, complete seriousness, and urgency. He thought that the pursuit of wisdom was the most important task for human beings. He thought that those of his fellow citizens who were after other goods were pursuing not wisdom but folly, and he let them know that he thought that through his elenctic arguments. I suspect that it was for this reason, at least as much as any other, that the Athenians tried, convicted, and executed him. Socrates described himself as a gadfly, and a gadfly is, from the perspective of the horse it bites, simply a pest. Enough Athenians thought Socrates a pest to bring about his death. They did what people everywhere do to irritating biting insects: they swatted him.

If Socrates was unfortunate in that he lived in a time when tempers were frayed, due to Athens' loss of the Peloponnesian War and the subsequent regime of the Thirty Tyrants, he was exceptionally fortunate in his followers. No philosopher ever had a more brilliant disciple than Plato, a philosopher of unsurpassed philosophical and literary gifts. It is largely because of Plato's dialogues that we remember Socrates as a great philosopher. There can be no doubt that the Socrates of Plato's dialogues has his roots in the Socrates of history. There can also be no doubt that Plato's portraits of Socrates go beyond the historical Socrates. Exactly where Socrates leaves off and Plato begins is a matter of disagreement among interpreters. Whatever else may be said of Socrates, his legacy includes the fact that he redirected the course of philosophy, virtually reinvented it: as Cicero said, he called philosophy down from the heavens and placed it in cities and homes. The questions he asked became the central questions of ancient ethics and not only Plato but also Aristotle and the Stoics acknowledge his influence on them. His intellectualist account of the good life, virtue, and vice influenced even those, like Plato and Aristotle, who rejected it. But more important than any doctrine that might be extracted from Plato's Socratic dialogues is the example of Socrates himself: fearless on trial, resolute in his pursuit of wisdom even at the cost of his life, and, despite his professions of ignorance, the "wisest and most just" man of his generation, as Plato puts it at the end of the *Phaedo*. He was, for Plato, the primary model of what a philosopher should be. He may not have been able to define the good life, but he lived it (at least in Plato's eyes; but also in the eyes of many philosophers since). Socrates is philosophy's martyr, and its saint.

# Plato

For Plato, Socrates was a liminal, transitional figure, who asked the Athenians to leave behind their traditional culture, but who could not reveal to them the full vision of which philosophy is capable. Plato does not resolve the paradox of Socrates in the *Republic*, perhaps his greatest work and a masterpiece of philosophy. He does, however, address it in a couple of ways. First, he gives an account of the virtues, which modifies the Socratic account in some respects but also keeps some of its essential features. Second, he offers an imaginative portrait of the good life that gives us an idea of what it would be like actually to attain wisdom. Socrates in the *Republic* continues to deny that he has knowledge, at least of the highest good; but he steps forth, in a way that goes way beyond what we have seen so far, in his willingness to offer a positive account of the good life. The *Republic* is a work on a large scale: it is divided into ten books. Only the *Laws*, Plato's final work, is longer. The official subject of the *Republic* is the nature of justice, which Socrates says is something "more precious than gold." Really, however, the question is whether the life of the just person is better or worse than the life of the unjust person; thus, the inquiry into justice concerns a "whole way of life." Socrates, of course, is the defender of the just life; the case for injustice is made first by Thrasymachus, a Sophist of the amoral, "realistic," cynical sort, whom I mentioned above, and then by Glaucon and Adeimantus, Plato's half-brothers.

Socrates begins his investigation of the just life with a couple of preliminary skirmishes, the first with an old man named Cephalus, in whose house the dialogue is set. Cephalus, an unreflective traditionalist, says that justice is telling the truth and paying one's debts; Socrates easily shows that there are exceptions to these "rules"—suppose someone had lent a weapon to you when in a sound mental state and now, deranged, asks you to return it? You would not tell him the truth and you would not give back the weapon. Evidently, justice can't be a matter of mere adherence to a set of rules, for rules will always have exceptions. When faced with Socrates' questions, Cephalus goes off "to look after the sacrifice"—the occasion of the dialogue is a religious festival—"bequeathing" his share in the argument to his son and heir, Polemarchus. Polemarchus is also a traditionalist: he relies on a saying of the poet Simonides, that justice is giving to each his due. Polemarchus adds that what is due to friends is something good, while what is due to enemies is harm. Socrates launches a variety of arguments against the latter claim, culminating in his famous rejection of the *lex talionis*, the law of retaliation ("an eye for an eye, a tooth for a tooth"): he says it is never right to harm another, or return evil for evil.

It is at this point in the discussion that Thrasymachus breaks in, in the manner of a blustering, belligerent bully—"like a wild beast," Plato says. He accuses Socrates of only asking questions but never answering. Persuaded to give his own answer to the question "What is justice?" Thrasymachus initially responds that justice is "the advantage of the stronger." This seems to imply a relativistic view of justice, as, by "the stronger," Thrasymachus means the rulers in different states: the wealthy in oligarchic regimes, the majority of the people in a democracy. When this claim fares badly under the Socratic elenchus, however, he switches to the view that injustice is "stronger, freer, and more masterly than justice," which reveals his own commitment to the "naturally superior individual," who is able to commit injustice and get away with it. This second position does no better under Socratic questioning. Book I of the dialogue ends in typical Socratic perplexity: Socrates accuses himself of trying to discover whether justice is preferable to injustice without first discovering what justice is.

The first book of the *Republic* reads like a typical Socratic dialogue, but in the rest of the *Republic* things take a different course. At the start of Book II, Plato's half-brothers, Glaucon and Adeimantus, enter the conversation, and Socrates talks mainly with them for the rest of the *Republic*. They claim that Socrates has not provided a convincing refutation of Thrasymachus. They don't believe Thrasymachus, but they want to be *really* convinced by Socrates that justice is preferable to injustice. They reformulate Thrasymachus' view, laying out the case for injustice. A memorable part of this is Glaucon's story of the Ring of Gyges. A Lydian shepherd, Gyges, discovers a ring in an underground tomb. When he becomes aware that the ring makes him invisible, he uses it to seduce the queen of the country, murder the king, and ascend to the throne. (Surely this is Thrasymachean injustice on a grand scale.) Anyone who possessed such a ring, Glaucon argues, would act as Gyges did; the only reason for refusing to act unjustly is fear of being caught. Glaucon and Adeimantus conclude their defense of injustice with a vivid portrait of an unjust man with a reputation for justice contrasted with a just man with a reputation for injustice. The former will become rich and powerful, forming alliances with whomever he wishes, while the latter will be unjustly accused, tortured and cruelly put to death. Glaucon and Adeimantus could hardly do a better job of articulating the conception of the person who acts in accordance with nature rather than convention, who wields power and successfully pursues pleasure. They are much better witnesses for this view than Thrasymachus, even though they don't believe it.

In the course of his defense of injustice, Glaucon presents a theory of justice that is *conventional*, though it is rooted in nature. People by nature don't like to suffer injustice at the hands of another, so they get together and establish laws and covenants to protect themselves against injustice. This is an early version of the social contract theory of justice, later developed by Hobbes and Locke. Socrates, in his defense of justice, substitutes for Glaucon's legalistic, conventionalist theory of justice a *naturalistic*, economic theory. Justice originates, he argues, because people are not self-sufficient: they need to cooperate to meet their basic needs. He founds a "city in speech," to illustrate this conception. The city is initially composed of four or five men, each of whom specializes in one area of production: a farmer, a shoemaker, a tailor, and a carpenter. Eventually, the city grows as luxuries are added along with specialists to obtain them. A class of "guardians" is introduced, which protects the ordinary citizens both from external enemies and internal predators. The guardians purify the city of its excesses, restoring natural order, as far as possible. This class is eventually divided into two: ruling guardians and auxiliaries, and with this division the city is complete. (Socrates calls this city *Kallipolis*, the "beautiful" or "fine" city.) What makes the city virtuous? It is wise because of the wisdom of its rulers, brave because of the courage of its auxiliaries, temperate because of the agreement of all on the question of who should rule, and just because everyone does the job that is suited to him. Next, Socrates adapts the account of the virtues to the individual. He divides the soul into three parts: reason, spirit, and appetite. Wisdom is the product of reason, courage of spirit, and temperance and justice of all three parts working together: temperance is the harmony of the parts of the soul; justice, their proper order. And now Thrasymachus can be answered: Socrates says that virtue is the mental health and well-being of the soul, while vice is disease, in our terms a mental illness; and who would not prefer health to illness?

This analysis of the virtues goes beyond anything we saw in the Socratic dialogues, in two ways. First, it is more detailed than the Socratic claim that virtue is knowledge. Second, it introduces parts of the soul, explains how they function, and associates the virtues with them. But the tripartite psychology allows the appetites or spirit, if they are sufficiently strong, to overpower reason, forcing an individual to act against what he or she knows to be best (moral weakness). This is a departure from pure Socratic intellectualism. So is the fact that three of the four virtues (courage, temperance, and justice) are defined in terms other than knowledge. Still, in the well-educated, moderate individual, reason does prevail over spirit and appetite, and justice is the result. Reason is not always in charge of every individual's life, as Socrates had thought, but it is in charge in the well-ordered life. It is the cause of the other virtues.

It would seem that Thrasymachus has been answered by the end of Book IV; justice has been proved to be superior to injustice. It turns out, however, that there is more to be said about the best life. Book IV tells us that the proper order of the soul is one with reason in control, and it follows from this that one function of reason is to order and control the lower parts of the soul, spirit and appetite. But there is another function of reason: to know the truth about reality. Ordering one's soul is just a precondition needed for its ultimate journey, to knowledge of the Good.

This journey is described in a long digression that makes up the central books of the *Republic*. Socrates takes up the subject because Glaucon raises a question about the possibility of *Kallipolis* ever coming into existence. It can't, Socrates answers, shocking Glaucon and probably everyone present, unless philosophers become kings or kings philosophers. Plato thought that all of our judgments of the qualities of the things that surround us are relative. Take beauty, for example: something that appears beautiful in one context or comparison will appear ugly, or at least not beautiful, in another. What Plato wanted, what Socrates before him had wanted, what they both thought the philosopher wants above all, is to find the universal, objective, and absolute standards on the basis of which our individual judgments are made. These standards he called Forms. I'll discuss the theory of Forms in chapter 2, and also the concept of knowledge that complements it. For the present, let me merely note that the life of the philosopher is a search for these Forms, and ultimately for the Form of the Good. These Forms are the objects of thought for which Socrates was seeking in the Socratic dialogues when he urged his interlocutors to think conceptually.

Plato thought that these Forms did not exist in the world around us, the world of relative judgments. Therefore, there must be another world, an "intelligible place," in which they could be found. The central books of the *Republic* describe the philosopher's search for that place and those Forms. The ultimate, most graphic and most memorable account of that search is the Allegory of the Cave, which begins Book VII. It is probably the best-known passage in all the dialogues, and maybe in all of philosophy. It begins with an image of prisoners in a cave, bound neck and foot, only able to look straight ahead at a wall before them, on which are projected moving images of objects. (If Plato had lived today, he would obviously have made use of movie theaters or rooms with big-screen televisions in his analogy.) These prisoners are completely absorbed in this "reality," and they converse by describing the "objects" they see. Behind these chained prisoners is a wall with a road behind it, along which other people carry the "originals" of which the chained prisoners only see the images. These "originals" are in fact themselves images of real objects in the world outside the cave, but neither the prisoners nor those carrying the objects know that. Behind all of this, projecting the shadows on the wall, is a fire. Now, if one of the chained prisoners were freed by someone and turned around, he would immediately see the "truth" about the images he had previously called real. This would surely be disorienting. And if he were then led up out of the cave, into the world above, he would find this even more disorienting. In fact, he would find it painful to be in the sunlight after being in the dark, and he would resist the ascent. Initially, he would be unable to discern anything in the upper world, but eventually, as his eyes adjusted, he would be able to see the real objects that were the true originals from which the copies in the cave were images. Finally, he would be able to see the sun, first in images (such as reflections in water), then directly. He would have obtained enlightenment, knowledge of the highest reality. Plato provides a key for the interpretation of the allegory, if one is needed: the cave stands for the sensible world, the upper world stands for the intelligible world, the fire stands for the sun and the sun stands for the Good. So now it becomes clear what the good life is (or at least the best life): it is the life in which one leaves the cave, the world of sensible objects, and enters the world of the Forms, ultimately seeing the Good. This is the life of the philosopher. This view grows out of the view of Socrates in the Socratic dialogues, who held that all of the virtues were forms of knowledge, and that knowledge of good and evil was the only exceptionless good. Still, the vividness and the apparent concreteness of the imagery of the cave take us far beyond the Socratic formulae. Few doubt that when we read this passage in the *Republic* we are in the realm of Plato's own thought.

Questions abound. How is this enlightenment attained? The allegory gives us the picture of an anonymous "someone" dragging the freed prisoner up and out of the cave by force. It is likely that the someone is supposed to represent Socrates leading others to philosophy. There certainly seems to be an allusion to Socrates later in the passage, when Plato describes the reaction of the prisoners to one who has attained enlightenment and returned to them, attempting to free them and lead them to the sunlight: "if they could somehow get their hands on him, wouldn't they kill him?" But Plato adds this: it is education that leads one out of the darkness of ignorance into the bright sunlight of knowledge; and education isn't a matter of putting sight into blind eyes, but of turning the soul around. Everyone has the capacity for this transformation, suggests Socrates; education takes the capacity for granted and works to turn the soul around to see the Good. Accordingly, there is an elementary education program in *Kallipolis* that focuses on love of the Beautiful (next of kin to the Good), followed by ten years of mathematical study, reserved for the future guardians and aimed at redirecting the soul away from the world of experience to abstract, conceptual reality, and culminating in five years of dialectic, leading to knowledge of the Good itself.

Why does the philosopher need to know the Good? Without knowledge of the Good, all of our ethical judgments are ultimately ungrounded, unjustified: if we don't know what the Good is, we can't know that the virtues we attempt to build into our character are in fact good. Without knowing the Good, we cannot judge correctly what is good. The philosopher, after attaining this knowledge, and *only* after attaining this knowledge, must go back down into the city and rule. (Remember, this long digression started with the claim that philosophers must become kings in the cities.) Ruling means making judgments about the shadows on the wall of the cave. But the philosopher will have an advantage that will enable him (or her; Plato expected there to be women guardians) to be able to see "ten thousand times" better than the cave dwellers, by virtue of knowing the standard of absolute Goodness and the other Forms. It is knowledge of the Good, and only that, that justifies the philosopher in ruling others.

But why would a philosopher who had come to know the Good even consider going back down into the cave? Wouldn't he or she much prefer to remain in the real world, the world of the Forms, and not descend into the world of falsehood, illusion? Wouldn't it be *unjust*, unfair, to force the philosopher to go back down into the cave? It is actually just, replies Socrates. The philosophers in a normal state would have attained enlightenment on their own. They would be entitled to remain in the upper world, contemplating the Forms and the Good. But the philosophers in *Kallipolis* have been educated by the state with the essential role of governing in mind, so they owe it to the state to return to the cave and govern, using their superior wisdom. They will fulfill this obligation, because it is just that they do so, and they are just people.

What exactly is the Good? Plato does not tell us. In this respect, despite the vividness of his portrait of the two worlds and the upward path, he leaves us in the same position of ignorance that Socrates claimed for himself. He denies that the Good is pleasure or knowledge. Perhaps the simplest answer is the least satisfying one: Good is Good, and that is the end of the matter. (The early twentieth-century philosopher G. E. Moore said something similar about "good" in his *Principia Ethica*.) Perhaps the Good cannot be explained in terms of other Forms because it is simple, incapable of being analyzed. Perhaps it has to be intuited, not known as a result of analysis. Perhaps the closest we can come to the Good is to talk about the philosopher's *experience* of the Good, and here too we must tread rather carefully over uncertain ground. The philosopher comes to know the Good by experiencing it in its participants, the other Forms, as in the *Symposium* the lover of Beauty comes to it by way of a ladder of ascent through various kinds of beautiful things. (Beauty and Goodness are very closely related for Plato, if not actually identical.) Somehow, as a result of the experience of the Good in its participants, the philosopher eventually is able to see the Good as it is in itself. Plato thinks of this experience as transformative, as life-changing.

Interpreters have seen in the philosopher's vision of the Good a mystical experience, in part because the experience is unanalyzable and thus inexpressible in terms of anything more basic, but also because of the image of (sun)light in the analogy. The difficulty with mystical experience is that it is impossible to say anything about it—it is ineffable. Plato later in Book VII suggests in discussing dialectic that the philosopher will come to be able to give an exact account of the Good, so perhaps the experience of the Good is not mystical in the sense of being strictly ineffable. But perhaps it is mystical in another sense. The ascent of the philosopher to the Good resembles the theist's ascent to God. God, for the theist, is—like the Good for the Platonic philosopher—the goal of a long search, a process of enlightenment. God is for the theist, as is the Good for the Platonist philosopher, the ultimate reality. For the theist to know God is to be happy, joyful, fulfilled. (St. Thomas Aquinas and others referred to the direct experience of God as the "beatific vision.") God, for the theist, is the ultimate source of and solution to the riddle of existence. If this comparison holds, it shows why, for Plato, to know the Good is to be in possession of knowledge that is ultimate, transformative, and explanatory.

It also shows why the life of the philosopher is the good life. The highest function of the rational part of the soul is to know reality. The Good is ultimate reality; it is what the rational part of the soul is made for. Thus, when the rational soul comes into contact with the Good, it perceives that this is the goal and completion of its search. Reason is only "at home" in the presence of genuine knowledge, not in the presence of the imitations that make up the bulk of our experiences. Thus, just as the soul of the theist is only happy in the presence of God, the soul of the Platonist philosopher is only happy in the presence of the Good. So, for Plato, the good life is the life of the philosopher. The philosopher contemplating the Form of the Good is Plato's most powerful image of the good life. (Not the philosopher down in the cave, ruling; the philosopher takes on that task reluctantly, out of necessity.) It is a portrait in the spirit of Socrates, faithful to the Socratic quest for moral knowledge, but it goes beyond anything Socrates said. It is based on the idea that the good life for the individual only depends on a single dimension: the attainment of knowledge. The other goods, such as those of the appetites and of spirit, are in the end just distractions. It is in one sense an extremely elitist model (we don't know for certain of anyone who has attained this goal; even in *Kallipolis*, with all the benefits of state education, the number of philosophers would be few) but in another sense it is democratic: Plato says that the soul of anyone could be turned to reality. The power is there for all, though only a few choose to develop and exercise it.

# Aristotle

The third philosopher in the developing conversation about the good life is Aristotle. Aristotle's *Nicomachean Ethics* is the most detailed, systematic treatment of ancient ethics that we possess. It is also the most influential: to many contemporary philosophers

## ARISTOTLE

Aristotle was born in Stagira, in Macedonia, in 384. His father, Nico-machus, was court physician to Amyntas III, the Macedonian king, who was the father of Philip of Macedon and the grandfather of Alexander the Great. In 367, when he was seventeen, he entered Plato's Academy, and remained there for twenty years, until Plato's death in 347. After Plato's death, Aristotle traveled in the Aegean, eventually settling in Lesbos, where he conducted many of his biological investigations. (Aristotle, in addition to being a great philosopher, was a great biologist, the first in the Western scientific tradition.) He married Pythias, the daughter of his friend Hermias, the ruler of Atarneus and a former member of Plato's Academy. They had a child, a girl named Pythias. In 342, he became the tutor of Philip's son Alexander. Later in life, after his wife died, he had a son, Nicomachus, by a former slave of Pythias, Herpyllis. The *Nico-machean Ethics* was written for him.

In 335, Aristotle returned to Athens and founded a school, the Lyceum. Most of the works in Aristotle's prodigious output prob-ably date to this time. He wrote dialogues, admired in antiquity for their style as well as their content; unfortunately, we have only fragments from these today. What survives are primarily what are known as treatises, which may have been Aristotle's lecture notes for classes in the Lyceum. He made major contributions to philoso-phy in all areas, including works in ethics, politics, the philosophy of nature, philosophical psychology, theology, and metaphysics. Aris-totle was the founder of symbolic logic and the first philosopher to study the formal validity of arguments. He wrote several works on logic, known collectively as the *Organon* ("instrument," presum-ably because logic is the instrument used in all thought).

Aristotle lived in Athens under the protection of Alexander. When Alexander died, in 323, anti-Macedonian sentiment led to his being charged with impiety, as Socrates and perhaps others had been. He left Athens for the nearby island of Euboeia, saying, "I will not allow Athens to sin twice against philosophy." His school, often called the "Peripatetic" school because Aristotle is said to have walked about while lecturing, had an "off and on" existence for several centuries. His works were lost for a time, then rediscovered in the first century BCE. They were edited (by Andronicus of Rhodes) and a number of his followers wrote commentaries on them. They were largely lost again in Western Europe when Rome fell in the fifth century CE, but were reintroduced to the West in the twelfth and thirteenth centuries via Islamic philosophers in Spain. At that time, they gained an unrivalled stature and influence: St. Thomas Aquinas often referred to Aristotle simply as "the Philosopher." They are still read today; the *Nicomachean Ethics* in particular is a standard text in ethics.

who adopt "virtue ethics" as their moral theory, it is the culminating work in ancient ethics. But it wasn't created out of nothing: Aristotle was writing in the tradition begun by Socrates and developed by Plato. Aristotle's years in the Academy shaped his views deeply, though he may never have fully accepted Plato's views. We can read Aristotle as a Platonist, though as a dissident one. Or we can read him as a Socratic, with his own answers to Socrates' questions; but we have to recognize that his answers are often very different from those Socrates suggested. Aristotle wrote at least two works on ethics, the *Eudemian Ethics* as well as the *Nicomachean*. I'll concentrate on the latter book in this work; it is by far the better known and more influential of the two. When I discuss Aristotle's "*Ethics*," it is the *Nicomachean Ethics* I'll be referring to.

I'll focus here, as with Plato, on Aristotle's account of the good life. The *Ethics* begins with a discussion of precisely that subject. Aristotle discusses three conceptions of the good life: the life of pleasure, the life of honor, and the life of the mind. When Aristotle talks about the life of pleasure, he does not mean the life of philosophy, which he later describes as the most pleasant of lives: he means the life spent in pursuit of the pleasures of food, drink, and sex. He dismisses this life as a life fit for cattle. Honor, Aristotle thinks, is obtained primarily through public life, but it depends on others, whereas he holds that *eudaimonia* is one's own possession, something that cannot be taken away by others, or by fate. A better answer would be the life of virtue, but even that is not quite right; it is not the mere possession of virtue, but its active exercise, that makes one *eudaimôn*. The life of wealth he dismisses in a sentence: wealth is not the end, but only a means to it. He also rejects Plato's idea that the good life is one spent in coming to know the Good. As he says, no one looks to the Good when practicing his art. Craftsmen look to the good relative to their art, or even to something less abstract and more particular. The doctor doesn't even look to the Form of Health in treating a patient, but to human health and even to some particular person's health.

That leaves the life of the mind. Aristotle argues that the good for a human being must be something final and self-sufficient: final in that we never desire it for the sake of something else, and self-sufficient in that if we have it we don't need anything else to live the good life. He argues further that the *ergon*, the "function" or the "work"—we might say the nature—of a human being, is the activity of the rational element of the soul. Though Aristotle does not use this precise phrase, the essence of his view of human nature is that "Man is a rational animal." The distinctively human life is one in which the rational element of the soul predominates. But there are two ways in which this may occur. First, one may devote one's life to the intellectual activity of contemplation, to science and philosophy, the attainment of what Aristotle refers to as theoretical wisdom. Contemplation, for Aristotle, is not the process of inquiry, especially not inquiry of a Socratic sort; rather, it is the understanding of a completed account of the nature of the world. It is not the *love* and pursuit of wisdom, but wisdom itself. Aristotle argues in Book X of the *Ethics* that this is the best life for a human being. Second, one may use one's reason to control the activity of the irrational part of the soul, the passions. This is the view articulated during most of the *Ethics*. (One can see in Aristotle's description of two lives a variation on Plato's two functions of reason in the *Republic*: the control of the appetites and emotions and the rational pursuit of the Good.) Reason, however, can function well or badly. To function well, it requires the virtues. Thus, it turns out that "the good of man is an activity of the soul in conformity with excellence or virtue, and if there are several virtues, in conformity with the best and most complete" (*E. N.* I.7, 1098a 16–18). Still, Aristotle states, we need what he calls "external goods" to live the good life, at least in the highest degree: friends, wealth, power, good birth, good children, and good looks. This insistence on the need for external goods in life conflicts with the life of Socrates: he was poor, without political power, and hardly handsome; yet his life was the model of the good life, both for Plato and later philosophers. The role of external goods in the good life will become a matter of controversy between Aristotle and the Stoics.

So there are two sorts of good life, according to Aristotle: the life of theoretical wisdom, of contemplation; and the life of practical wisdom, for instance a life spent in political activity. You might think here of the life of Albert Einstein and the life of Abraham Lincoln. In Book X of the *Ethics*, as I mentioned above, Aristotle argues that the life of theoretical wisdom is preferable to the life of practical wisdom. Theoretical wisdom deals with the highest things in the universe, including the Unmoved Mover, Aristotle's God; whereas practical wisdom deals with human affairs. Theoretical wisdom is something that is under one's control—Aristotle says it is "leisurely"—whereas practical wisdom depends on the actions of others. Masters of practical wisdom must respond to crises, which in general are not of their own making. Aristotle thinks that theoretical wisdom may be practiced in isolation, whereas the life of practical wisdom requires the cooperation of others. Einstein could think alone in his study at Princeton, but Lincoln needed his cabinet, his congress, and his generals to win the American Civil War. Aristotle thinks the life of contemplation more *pleasant* than the life of practical wisdom; at the very least, he says, the life of contemplation holds pleasures "marvelous in their purity and certainty." All in all, the life of contemplation is divine rather than human, though that does not mean that human

beings ought not to pursue it. Just because the life of contemplation is superior to the life of practical wisdom, however, that does
not disqualify the life of practical wisdom as a form of the good
life. Both lives are rational lives, and the active, virtuous exercise
of reason is what makes a life good for a human being.

Aristotle's view of the best life differs somewhat from Plato's,
though it also contains similarities. Because Aristotle divides
theoretical and practical reason, he makes contemplation a purely
theoretical activity, devoid of moral content, and confines moral
activity to our composite, human nature. Because Plato does
not divide the two aspects of reason, and because he sees the
object of reason as a specifically moral one, namely the Good,
reason is thoroughly moral for Plato, from contemplation of the
Good down to life in the human world of the cave. But both
agree that the highest form of rational activity is divine, and that
it is something humans possess in virtue of a divine, immortal
aspect of their souls. They also agree that the best human life is
the one in which this rational activity is found: the life of the
philosopher.

It is perhaps surprising that, given his preference for the
life of contemplation over the life of practical wisdom, Aristotle spends the bulk of the *Ethics* discussing the latter rather than
the former. The work is concerned with ethics, however, and
ethics is concerned with practical wisdom. But what is practical
wisdom? (The Greek word is *phronêsis*; the person who possesses
it is called the *phronimos*.) It is wisdom in the realm of action. That
is, it is concerned with things we *do*, whereas contemplation is
concerned with things outside our power, such as the nature of
the heavens. Aristotle distinguishes three kinds of reason:

1) Theoretical reason, involved in contemplation and concerned
   with what is unchangeable and thus not in our power to control.
2) Art, or productive reason, concerned with things we *make*.
3) Practical reason, concerned with what we *do*.

A carpenter, a shipbuilder, a tailor, and artisans in general all possess a kind of expert knowledge of their art. But just as the artisan knows how to make things, the *phronimos* knows what to do in certain particular concrete situations. Though Aristotle distinguishes the *phronimos* from the artist, he does not distinguish the ethically excellent individual from one who excels in politics. Ethics and politics have the same end, the attainment of the good life: the private individual seeks the good life for himself, whereas the politician seeks it for everyone in his city. What characterizes the wise individual in both the private and the public spheres is practical wisdom. Ultimately, this wisdom involves intuition about what is required in some particular situation. At a crisis point in the American Civil War, when England and France were considering recognizing the government of the Confederacy, Lincoln issued the Emancipation Proclamation, freeing the slaves in the seceding states. He made explicit the fact that the war was not primarily about the preservation of the Union but about slavery. The Proclamation was of dubious legality, but it was also a political masterstroke; it made it virtually impossible for other nations to give support to the Confederacy. It is decisions like this that mark Lincoln and other great statesmen as *phronimoi*, men of practical wisdom.

In Aristotle's view, there are two kinds of virtue: there is moral virtue, which is formed by habit; and there is intellectual virtue, which is formed by teaching. Practical wisdom is an *intellectual* virtue, but one that involves the moral virtues. Practical wisdom is concerned with making good choices, choices that lead to, or are partially constitutive of, *eudaimonia*. Specifically, it is concerned with the reasoning process that precedes our choice of a particular action. This reasoning process is known as deliberation. Practical wisdom, for Aristotle, is the art of deliberating well. But deliberation is the rational determination of the best means to a particular end. What ensures that the end is good? In Aristotle's view, it is not our ability to deliberate, but our character. If our character is good—if we possess the moral virtues—we will have the correct ends. If our character is bad, we will have bad ends, and even if we reason well about attaining those ends, we will not be practically wise. Aristotle calls the ability to reason well about any end whatsoever "cleverness." Practical wisdom is the ability to reason well about good ends, and it is moral virtue that gives the *phronimos* good ends.

Let's see how this works in practice. Consider the citizen soldier, standing in formation and preparing to face the onslaught of an enemy army. Let's suppose that this particular soldier desires to protect his homeland and family. That is, he has a virtuous desire. (A soldier who had no concern for anyone but himself would already be planning his escape.) But if he has not been properly habituated to face these situations, he may respond in one of two non-virtuous ways. He may see the enemy host as larger and more powerful than it actually is, and his chances of survival as less. He may be overcome by fear and he may, as a result, bolt from his position in line and run away. In ordinary situations, this is called cowardice. Or he may be convinced of his own invulnerability, and he may leave his formation and advance alone against the enemy, challenging their best soldier to single combat. The heroes in Homer's *Iliad* behave in this way. For Achilles, the greatest of the Greek heroes, this behavior would not be foolish, but for others, and let's include in this group our citizen soldier, it would be. One soldier is led by an excess of fear to over-estimate the danger to himself and thus to run away; the other is led by an excess of confidence to underestimate that danger and to behave rashly. Neither cowardice nor rashness is a virtue. Whether I am rash or cowardly, Aristotle believes, is determined by a lifetime of facing similar situations and acting well or badly in each of them. That is, it is determined by habit. If I have formed the right habits, I will perceive what is called for in the situation correctly, neither exaggerating nor underestimating its features, and I will act accordingly.

Practical wisdom is, as I have said, an intellectual virtue, but one that requires the moral virtues. The moral virtues, in turn, require practical wisdom. Every moral virtue, Aristotle thinks, is a mean between two extremes, just as we saw in the case of courage, rashness, and cowardice above. But how is that mean determined? It is determined by the *phronimos*. Moral virtue, as Aristotle defines it, is "a characteristic involving choice, and ... it consists in observing the mean relative to us, a mean which is defined by a rational principle, such as a *man of practical wisdom* would use to determine it" (*E. N.* II.6, 1106b36–1107a2). How is moral virtue acquired? By following the guidance of the *phronimos*. The *phronimos* will tell us what choices are correct for us, in our situations. How do we become autonomous moral agents? By becoming *phronimoi* ourselves. If we get our moral education from cowards, we become cowards; if we get it from rash people, we become rash. "Hence it is no small matter," Aristotle writes, "whether one habit or another is inculcated in us from early childhood; on the contrary, it makes a considerable difference, or, rather, all the difference" (*E. N.* II.1, 1103b 23–25).

Clearly, in order for moral education to work, we must be able to identify the *phronimos*. In one way, this is easy; in another, it is difficult, or perhaps even impossible. Every culture, I suppose, contains individuals who embody to a high degree the moral standards of their society, who are held up by everyone as exemplars of moral virtue or practical wisdom. It is not difficult to find such people and learn from them. But what if the standards of a given society are in fact immoral? Here the *phronimos* would have to be the rare, courageous individual who stands up to immorality. And how would that society's moral standards and practices make it possible for a *phronimos* to arise? Socrates sought culturally invariant, universal moral virtues; Plato described a process whereby the philosopher might rise above the culture of the cave and discover the Good. Is Aristotle's *phronimos* similarly one who seeks the universal in moral conduct? Or is he bound to be shaped definitively by the standards prevalent in his society? It is not difficult to identify *phronimos*-figures in a small, traditional society in which there is widespread agreement about the correct moral values. But, assuming that Socrates was in fact an example of the *phronimos*, it proved impossible for a majority of the jurors at his trial to identify him as such. In a society that is divided, or even worse, fragmented, as modern society appears to be, identification of the *phronimos* is no easy task. But if we cannot identify the *phronimos* we cannot know what the standard of virtue is, because that standard is defined in terms of the *phronimos*.

Moral virtue is defined by Aristotle in terms of correct choices, choices that "hit the mean" between excess and deficiency. But this makes moral virtue sound too intellectual. Moral virtue involves choice, and we are in control of our choices, so why can't everyone observe the mean all the time? The answer is that our emotions interfere with our choices, and, if we have been habituated, trained, to feel excessively or deficiently in various cases, we will not perceive the mean that the *phronimos* perceives. Each soldier in the example above probably believes that he is acting correctly. The coward believes that running away is the right thing to do, and that all of those who stay in formation are foolishly sacrificing their lives. The reckless soldier believes that those who stay in formation are really cowards, that the thing to do is to get out in front and fight. In other situations, involving other virtues, the self-indulgent person systematically overestimates the contribution that piece of chocolate cake would make to his or her happiness and under-estimates its effect on his or her waistline. The stingy person believes that the right amount to give to charity is a pittance, whereas the *phronimos* judges, correctly, that a more generous amount is called for. We cannot alter the conduct of those who are not virtuous by arguing with them about the location of the mean on the vice–virtue continuum; we need to alter their habits. That is why early childhood education is so important. In this respect also, Aristotle's view resembles Plato's in the *Republic*.

As a eudaimonist, Aristotle tends to emphasize the value of virtue to the life of the individual possessing it. There are two cases, however, where virtue positively requires the recognition of the welfare of others: justice and friendship. Aristotle defines justice as "the good of another" (*E. N.* V.1, 1130a 3–4) and says that "alone of all the virtues" it is concerned with the welfare of others. "The best man," says Aristotle, "is not one who practices virtue toward himself, but who practices it toward others, for that is a hard thing to achieve. Justice in this sense, then, is not a part of virtue but the whole of excellence or virtue" (*E. N.* V.1, 1130a 7–10). The kind of justice Aristotle is talking about here is what he calls "complete justice." There are two kinds of partial justice: justice in the distribution of benefits and justice in the rectification of wrongs. Because justice proceeds in accordance with general rules, or laws, it must be supplemented by equity, which deals with individual cases. The just person in all contexts is the one who follows the correct rules in dealing with other people; the unjust person is the one who favors himself when goods are to be distributed and seeks to avoid punishment when rectification is in order.

If the ethical standard is one's own happiness, why should one seek another's good by practicing justice? Aristotle does not answer this question directly in his discussion of justice, but two answers suggest themselves from what he says elsewhere. The first is that human beings are political animals, and have need of one another. Human beings are not self-sufficient; they are meant by nature for life in society, and only flourish there. "One's own good cannot exist without household management nor without a political system" (*E. N.* VI.8, 1142a 9–10). A person who did not have need of others, who could live outside the *polis*, the city, would be either a beast or a god. The second answer is that to live virtuously is to live in accordance with practical reason, and the principles of justice are principles of practical reason. Therefore, it would be irrational to act contrary to justice. If justice is one virtue that positively requires consideration of others, another is friendship. Aristotle considers three kinds of friendships: those based on pleasure, utility, and virtue. The highest form of friendship is that based on virtue, and in a virtue-based friendship one values a friend not (only) for the pleasure they bring or their usefulness, but for their own sake. Friendship is based on self-love: "all friendly feelings toward others are an extension of the friendly feelings a person has for himself" (*E. N.* IX.8, 1168b 6–7). Accordingly, "a man is his own best friend and therefore should have the greatest affection for himself" (*E. N.* IX.8, 1168b 9–10). Does this make human nature egoistic? Yes and no. Aristotle notes that we condemn as egoists those who seek to gratify their own appetites and emotions. Those who seek to gratify their intellect and to act in accordance with virtue, as do friends of the best sort, are never considered egoists; "however, it would seem that such a person is actually a truer egoist or self-lover. At any rate, he assigns what is supremely noble and good to himself, he gratifies the most sovereign part of himself, and he obeys it in everything" (*E. N.* 1168b 28–31). In valuing virtue, both in himself and in his friend, the good person values what is best in himself, his "true self," his intellect rather than his emotions or appetites. It is in this sense that a virtuous friend is another self. (I should note in this context that the Greek word for friendship, *philia*, includes family relations as well as voluntary associations. One's spouse, one's children, one's parents are "friends," hopefully in the best sense of the term.)

One might think that the value of practical wisdom was as a means to the good life. This is not the case. Since the good life is the life of virtue, and since the intellectual virtues are better than the moral virtues, because the intellect is a higher part of the soul than the appetites and emotions, it is more accurate to say that the good life just *is* the life of reason. Even that is not quite accurate, however: Aristotle regards external goods, such as "good birth, good children and beauty," as essential at least for "supreme happiness." The question of external goods aside,

however, Aristotle would say that the life of practical wisdom was
(one form of) the happy life.

# After Aristotle: the Stoics and Epicureans

The death of Aristotle in 322, one year after the death of Alexander, is often seen as a watershed in the history of philosophy.
At that time there were two schools of philosophy in Athens: the
Academy, founded by Plato, and Aristotle's Lyceum. A quarter of
a century later, there were four. The new schools were *Epicurus'*
*"Garden,"* and *Zeno of Citium's "Stoa."* These new schools ushered
in a period known as the "Hellenistic" era in philosophy. (This
term is borrowed from history, where it denotes the period from
the death of Alexander in 323 to the defeat of Marc Antony and
Cleopatra by Octavian—later Augustus—at the battle of Actium
in 31, which marked the beginning of the Roman Empire.)
Though it is true that these schools bring new voices to the
conversation, one may wonder to what degree they truly constitute a new era of philosophy. Stoicism owes a considerable debt
to the philosophy and personal inspiration of Socrates and to the
philosophy of Plato, and both schools engaged in conversation
with their older rivals. (The Academy changed its orientation in
the third century, partly in response to the rise of Stoicism, and
became skeptical in outlook, following the model of Socrates.)
If philosophy changed in some decisive way when Stoicism
and Epicureanism came on the scene, later writers don't seem
to notice: they treat philosophy as a continuous tradition, dating
back to the Presocratics and Socrates. Consider as an example
Cicero's philosophical works, written during the last three years
of his life (46–43), which are mainly dialogues among Academic,
Peripatetic, Stoic, and Epicurean philosophers, put in the mouths
of various illustrious Romans. There is no hint in these dialogues

that philosophy somehow changes its character with the death of Aristotle.

There *were* historical developments that affected the course of philosophy after Aristotle's death. In 155, the Athenians sent an embassy of three philosophers (a Stoic, an Academic, and a Peripatetic) to Rome on a political mission. This embassy created quite a stir, and aroused interest among the Romans, not all of it favorable, in philosophy. In 86, the Roman strongman Sulla sacked Athens and destroyed the sites of the philosophical schools, causing a dispersal of philosophy from its traditional home. (Alexandria in Egypt, a center of intellectual activity of all kinds and home of the ancient world's greatest library, and eventually Rome became new centers of philosophy.) During this period, thanks initially to the work of Cicero and Lucretius, philosophy came to be written in Latin as well as Greek, and as a result became widely accessible in the western part of the Empire. Though the Romans brought a practical bent to the study of philosophy, they did not abandon the more theoretical aspects of the subject. In about 176 CE, the Roman Emperor Marcus Aurelius, himself an important Stoic philosopher, established four chairs of philosophy, one for each of the schools, in Athens, in recognition of the city's status as the traditional home of philosophy and of the continuing vitality of the schools. The debate among the four schools, with other voices joining in, lasted into the third century CE, when a revived Platonism became dominant, sweeping all before it, and forming the basis of the Christian theology of Augustine. (The last period is beyond the scope of this book.)

There were also, doubtless, some changes in the character of philosophy in this period. The political changes brought about by the rise, first, of the Macedonian Empire of Philip II and his son Alexander, and later the Roman Empire, inevitably had an effect on the moral and political philosophy of these schools—no longer could philosophy take the autonomous, independent city-state as the model of political organization; rather, one had to take the existence of great empires into account. Perhaps because of these political changes philosophers begin to think of the end of life, its purpose or goal, as a kind of inner peace, tranquility. Philosophy in this period is often said to be *therapeutic* in character, as providing a cure for the disorders brought about by life in the imperial world. Stoicism and Epicureanism became *popular* philosophies; they performed a function now performed primarily by religion, that of offering an account of the meaning of life. In the words of religious writer and scholar Karen Armstrong, "Nobody expected religion to ... provide an answer to the meaning of life. People turned to philosophy for that kind of enlightenment." Still, the therapy is cognitive in character: the attainment of wisdom is held by both Stoics and Epicureans to be essential to attaining tranquility. One had to *think* one's way into Stoicism or Epicureanism. Stoicism and Epicureanism, though they are polar opposites in some respects, are very similar in others. Both agreed that the aim of life was the attainment of inner peace, tranquility, a state of being unperturbed in the face of challenges from the outside world. Neither school had any use for luxury (the popular understanding of Epicureanism is completely erroneous on this point). They both defended the virtues as essential to the good life, though they understand the relation between virtue and the good life differently. Both schools are *dogmatic*, in that they offer specific doctrines as the basis of their philosophy; and both schools are *materialistic*, in that they think that everything that exists, including God or the gods and the soul, is made of some kind of stuff. Both divide philosophy into three branches: canonic, physics, and ethics for the Epicureans; and logic, physics, and ethics for the Stoics. Beyond these points of agreement differences emerge.

## Stoicism

Let's consider the Stoics first.

## STOICISM

Stoicism originates with Zeno of Citium, who was born about 331 BCE and died about 262. He began teaching in Athens about 301, at the "Painted Colonnade" (*Stoa Poikilê*), from which the school derived its name. Stoicism is in some respects similar to the philosophy of the Cynics (literally, "doglike" philosophers), who flouted convention in an attempt to live "in accordance with nature." The Stoics adopted the goal of the Cynics, but not their extreme behavior. Like Epicurean atomism, Stoicism was a materialist philosophy; unlike Epicureanism, it underwent considerable development over the centuries, in part because of debate with the Academic Skeptics. We may think of Stoicism as being divided into three distinct periods: an early period, when it was centered in Athens, a transitional middle period, and a later, Roman period. The early Stoics include, in addition to Zeno, Cleanthes of Assos (who died in 232), whose "Hymn to Zeus" is the only complete work we have from the period, and Chrysippus of Soli (who died in 206), considered the "second founder" of the school. We have only fragments of the works of Zeno and Chrysippus, despite the fact that the latter is said to have written over seven hundred works.

Later Stoicism is sometimes referred to as "Imperial Stoicism," because it flourished in the Roman Empire. Cicero, an Academic by conviction, features Stoic philosophy prominently in his philosophical works. Several Stoic philosophers lived and wrote in this period, and unlike the earlier Stoics we possess several complete works from three of them. The first of the three, Seneca, who lived from about 1 BCE to 65 CE, served as an advisor to the Roman Emperor Nero. Eventually, Nero forced him to commit suicide because of suspicions that he had been involved in a plot against his life. He is best known in philosophical circles for a number of essays and a collection of 124 letters to his friend Lucilius, which are themselves really short essays on Stoic philosophy. Epictetus (who lived from about 55 to about 135) was a freed slave who wrote nothing himself. His thoughts were recorded by his disciple Arrian in a collection entitled *Discourses*. A brief selection from the *Discourses* can be found in Epictetus' *Manual* or *Handbook*. While Seneca wrote in Latin, Epictetus (Arrian) and the Roman Emperor Marcus Aurelius (121–180) wrote in Greek. The work we call the *Meditations* was originally Marcus' diary, entitled simply "to himself." Seneca, Epictetus, and Marcus Aurelius all emphasize the ethical aspects of Stoicism, which they treat as a way of life. The classic works of these authors have been the major source of knowledge of Stoicism among educated Europeans, not just philosophers, for centuries. They remain the "public face" of Stoicism even today for many to whom the original Stoics—Zeno, Cleanthes, Chrysippus— are little more than names.

We come to Stoicism, before we even read any Stoic authors, with a rough idea of what the Stoic philosophy is like, simply because of our terms "stoical" and "stoic." To be stoical is to be stolid and unwavering in enduring all forms of adversity. As an initial approximation, this is not altogether misleading, but let's try to place the idea of unwavering endurance in historical context. According to one of the earliest Stoic formulae, the aim of life is to live "in agreement," which was expanded to "in agreement with nature." What this means is that, when you are faced with challenges from the world that exist beyond the limits of your will, you must accept what nature requires of you. One of the most vivid Stoic analogies designed to illustrate this point is that of a dog tied to a cart. When the cart begins to move, the dog faces a choice: he may either trot along beside the cart cheerfully, or resist the force of the cart pulling him forward. Either way the dog is going to follow the cart, but only in the first case is the dog "in accordance" with nature. Another name for "nature" here is "fate." When faced with fate, you can either lament your lot or live harmoniously with what fate has determined for you.

What is it that enables one to live in accordance with nature? Virtue—and virtue is wisdom. The virtuous person, the wise person, is the one who understands that he or she must accept what fate has determined for his or her life. The person who has achieved this wisdom is called the *sage*. The sage is the Stoic counterpart of the Platonic philosopher-king or the Aristotelian *phronimos*. Like these two figures, the sage is an ideal, probably an unrealizable one. The sage's alignment of his or her will to nature is perfect, infallible. As a result, he or she attains tranquility. Since the attainment of tranquility is all that matters in life, wisdom—virtue—is the only good. Wisdom is not simply a means to tranquility; rather, the life of wisdom is literally the good life. Wisdom may appear in different contexts, and in those contexts it may be called by different names: wisdom in contexts where one might feel fear is courage; wisdom in contexts where one might be tempted by pleasure is called temperance; wisdom regarding what other humans are due is justice, and so on. At bottom, though, all of the virtues are forms of wisdom, and wisdom is the knowledge of how to align one's will with nature.

Ordinary people, those of us who are not sages, act on occasion on the basis of reason, but much of the time we act on the basis of emotion. The Stoics thought that an emotion was essentially a *mistaken judgment* about what is good. We think that things like good looks, health, long life, prosperity, family connections, a happy family life, and so on, are intrinsically good. We are emotionally attached to them. According to the Stoics, these things are neither good nor bad in themselves, but *indifferent*. Most Stoics thought that some indifferents were "preferred," and others "dispreferred," but that did not make them good or bad. In this respect, they differed from Socrates: he thought that these things were good *if* they were guided by wisdom, but otherwise not. That is, he thought of them as *conditional* goods. Aristotle divided goods into three classes: external goods, goods of the body, and goods of the soul. He thought that some external goods were necessary for a happy life, or at least for a supremely happy life. The Stoics disagreed. We might think this disagreement only verbal: what the Stoics called "preferred" Socrates called "conditionally good." Cicero, in fact, complains that this is only a difference in terminology. I think, however, that it is not. If all I need to be happy is tranquility, I can be happy under any circumstances, even when dying of thirst or hunger, provided that I accept this fate as due to nature. Of course I would *prefer* to be well fed, healthy, and prosperous, but will my possession of these "goods" enhance the goodness of my life? It is a cliché, but a useful one, to note that Stoicism is a philosophy for people in any walk of life, from slaves (e.g. Epictetus) to emperors (e.g. Marcus Aurelius). Happiness, according to the Stoics, is simply a matter of understanding nature correctly, and that understanding is equally available to people from the lowest to the highest strata of society.

To see why the Stoics think that virtue is the only good, necessary and sufficient attribute for living the good life, consider the following. Imagine that I am trying to decide which of three biographies to read, and that I am looking in particular for a biography of someone I can admire and perhaps even emulate. The first is a biography of a person who had every advantage in life: wealth, power, good looks, and family connections— all the Stoic "preferred indifferents"—and who used these advantages to amass more wealth and power, generally by unscrupulous means. Imagine that this person had no true friends, only sycophants who constantly flattered him. Everyone recognized that this was a person to be feared, but everybody also recognized that he was a bad person. The second is a biography of a person who likewise had every advantage in life, but who put those advantages to work in developing an excellent character. He treated others with justice and benevolence, he was honest and upright, and he had many friends who loved him. But his life went smoothly, with a minimum number of obstacles to face, few "bumps in the road." Imagine that he was fortunate and achieved a level of success comparable to that of the first person. It is clear which biography describes the life of a better, more admirable person, a more suitable subject for emulation. Now consider the biography of a third person, who had none of those advantages: born into poverty, with no family connections, unattractive in appearance, suffering from ill health, living under a repressive political regime with no chance of personal advancement, perhaps even in prison, but who nonetheless developed a virtuous character. Suppose this person had to overcome huge obstacles in life just to survive, but who endured all of the trials that life sent his way. We might *prefer* it if our lives resembled the life of the second person rather than the third, but do we want to say that the life of the second person was more *admirable*, more worthy of approval, than the third's? Might we not think that the third person, just because he had to overcome such obstacles, led a life that was in some way *better* than that lived by the other two? Or even if we would not go that far, might we not find the third person's biography more edifying than that of the others? That is what the Stoics meant by calling such things as health, wealth, good looks, good birth, etc., "preferred indifferents" rather than goods, even conditional goods. They are nice additions to a life, but they do not make a life more virtuous, more admirable, or in a word, better. If I can acquire them and keep my self-respect, trustworthiness and high-mindedness, as Epictetus says about wealth, then by all means let me acquire them; but not if they require me to sacrifice my character.

The life of the ordinary person, the non-sage, is a life guided by mistaken judgments about what is good—that is, by false values. The sage, on the other hand, is infallible in understanding what is good. When the ordinary person sets out on a course of action, he or she says, "I want to attain this goal." The sage says, "I want to attain this goal, but primarily I want to keep my mind in accordance with nature." This brings up a problem. Can anyone actually be the sage? Has a sage ever existed? Was Epictetus a sage? Marcus Aurelius? The Stoics often talked as though there were sages in our midst, but they also had to admit that they could not name an actual historical example, unless Socrates might have qualified. But Socrates professed ignorance, and the sage had to be wise. Where does that leave the rest of us? The early Stoics had a particularly harsh view of this matter. If you were not the sage, your life was wretched. Not only that, but all defective lives were equally wretched. The person who constantly strove for sagehood, only to fall the slightest bit short, was no better off than the worst tyrant of history. If you were drowning, they argued, it did not matter whether you were drowning in a few feet of water or in the ocean depths. And yet ... the Stoics used the concept of "making progress" to describe the student of Stoic philosophy. It is hard to see how Stoicism could have been such a popular philosophy if it had not held out hope to its followers for the attainment of the good life.

This account of Stoic ethics is far from complete; it must be connected to the Stoic accounts of knowledge (and, in particular, of deliberation), the soul, and nature. I'll make those connections in later chapters. Before I turn to the rival account of the good life offered by the Epicureans, however, I want to mention two features of Stoic ethics—their account of justice, and their approval, under certain conditions, of suicide. Like Socrates, Plato, and Aristotle, the Stoics were eudaimonists, and eudaimonism begins with the assumption that we care for our own well-being, that we desire to live the good life ourselves. How do we get from this concern to concern for the well-being of others? The Stoic response is to remove the individual from the evaluative center of the universe. When we judge in accordance with our emotions, we give pride of place to our own situation: *our* pain, *our* pleasure, *our* hope, *our* fear. When we look at things rationally, though, we see no reason to think that our own well-being is somehow a special case in the big picture of things. We are ultimately forced by reason to think of the well-being of each person in the world as equally important. That is the basis of the Stoic theory of justice, which gave rise to the idea of *cosmopolitanism*, the idea that we are ultimately "citizens of the world," the cosmos. This has proved to be one of the most enduring and attractive aspects of Stoic ethics.

On the other hand, the Stoic approval of suicide (a favorite topic of Seneca, in particular) seems at odds with their general view of the good life as life in accord with nature. Ordinarily, the Stoics admit, life promises an excess of good over evil. There are occasions, however, where future prospects appear to be grim—and not just to the ordinary person, but to the sage. Under those circumstances, one might choose to commit suicide, just as one might choose to leave a smoke-filled room. This seems problematic in two respects. First, if nothing is good but virtue, if virtue is indifferent to circumstance, and if nothing can shake the virtue of the sage, what future situations would influence him or her to commit suicide? Granted, the sage will not value continued life, or longevity, itself: that would be an indifferent, even if a preferred one. Still, why should the sage be influenced by the possibility of a future filled with similar conditions, which could at best be indifferents also? Second, isn't the choice to kill oneself in the face of oncoming bad events (think, perhaps, of a spy choosing to take cyanide rather than to face torture) an attempt to alter the course of nature, rather than to live in accordance with it? The Stoics would argue that the choice of suicide in such circumstances would be in accord with nature, since nature was heading in the direction of certain death anyway, but it still seems that by killing oneself one would be interfering with the future course of events. Suicide was a fact of life in Seneca's time. The emperors forced many of their enemies to kill themselves. Seneca himself was forced by Nero to kill himself, as I mentioned above. The Stoics held up as a hero the younger Cato, who committed suicide in 46 BCE rather than submit to the rule of Julius Caesar. Still, it seems difficult to reconcile the practice of suicide with the other Stoic doctrines mentioned above.

## Epicureanism

Let's turn now from Stoicism to Epicureanism.

### EPICUREANISM

Epicurus (341–270) was the child of Athenian parents, and thus an Athenian citizen, who grew up on the island of Samos. In 306, he established his school at his home not far from the Academy. The school is called the "Garden," because Epicurus met with his followers in the garden of his home. Epicurus was a prolific writer, producing in his lifetime over three hundred scrolls. As in the case of the early Stoics, however, we have only a small portion of his work: three letters, preserved by Diogenes Laertius, and two collections of his central doctrines. This sad fact is compensated for, if not completely, by an epic poem of six books in Latin by the Roman poet Lucretius, *On the Nature of Things*, which summarized Epicurus' physical theory. As in the case of the Stoics, Cicero included Epicureanism in his philosophical dialogues, though he does not always display it in the most attractive light. There is a library of over three hundred scrolls belonging to the Epicurean philosopher Philodemus from a villa at Herculaneum destroyed by the eruption of Vesuvius in 79 CE; unfortunately, these scrolls are burned so badly that it has been impossible to read most of them. As I write this, however, new technology has been developed that could make it possible to read these charred remains. If that proves correct, it could revolutionize our understanding of Epicureanism. From what we know at present, however, Epicureanism, unlike Stoicism, does not seem to have undergone much development over time. Epicurus was venerated by his students (Lucretius calls him a god and the savior of humankind) and it is likely that his writings were treated as something akin to holy scripture, not to be tampered with.

I noted above some similarities between Stoicism and Epicureanism. For the most part, however, the two schools are opposites. The Stoics think the good is life in accordance with nature; for Epicurus, the good is pleasure. By "pleasure," however, he does not mean what comes first to most people's minds: the pleasures of eating, drinking, and sex. Another ancient school, the Cyrenaics, adopted the pursuit of these pleasures as their good, but the Epicureans were careful to distinguish themselves from them. (This is why our term "epicure" for the person who pursues, in particular, the pleasures of fine food and drink is completely misleading when applied to Epicurus.) The Epicureans referred to these as "kinetic" pleasures—pleasures involving bodily motion. Eating and drinking are responses to hunger and thirst, which are natural and necessary desires, so it is inevitable that people spend some time satisfying them. We might think of kinetic pleasures as dynamic, episodic: they are only experienced while eating or drinking, and so on. (Epicurus thought sexual pleasure natural but not necessary; he thought one could live without it.) They generally find the replenishment process of eating when hungry and drinking when thirsty pleasant. But there is another kind of pleasure, which the Epicureans called "static" or "stable" pleasure, which occurs when the pain of hunger and thirst is satisfied. Epicurus defines this state of satisfaction as the absence of pain, which makes it sound as if pleasure was no sensation at all. Epicurus' view may have been as simple as that; certainly Cicero thought it was. He objected that no one but an Epicurean would call this absence of sensation pleasant, and argued that Epicurus did not know the meaning of the word. I am not sure that this is a fair objection. Though the Epicureans talked as if static pleasure was simply the absence of pain, Plutarch (like Cicero, a critic of Epicureanism) refers to it as a "comfortable" sensation, and it might not be too much of a stretch to think of it as a positive state of satisfaction that occurs when we are not afflicted with pain of any sort. If so, this general state of satisfaction, thought of as a stable mental state, might be seen as a static pleasure—the pleasure, in fact, that attends on a life of psychological peace, tranquility, and freedom from anxiety.

The enemies of a pleasant, tranquil life are physical pain and anxiety. To some extent, physical pain is unavoidable; but Epicurus says that chronic pain is bearable and acute pain is over quickly. Epicurus' followers cited as proof of this statement the fact that he endured his own last days, which were very painful, with cheerful calm. But to some extent the amount of pain we experience is under our control. We can minimize our pain by limiting desire to objects that are readily obtainable. Inexpensive food and drink satisfy hunger and thirst as well as fine food and wine. Luxuries such as these may not be always available; but if we practice moderation, training our appetites to be content with simple food and drink, we can not only satisfy our hunger and thirst but also remove our anxiety about obtaining

gourmet food and fine wine in the future. As I noted above, the
Epicureans thought that sexual desire was "natural but unnecessary." Epicurus thought, reasonably enough, that sexual desire led
to marriage, and marriage led to children. Both were anxiety-
producing and in his mind ought to be avoided, for the sake of
mental tranquility. The same goes for such "unnatural" desires as
the desire for fame and fortune. Unlike the Stoics, who endorsed
political activity (a stance particularly congenial to the Romans,
who were very civic-minded), the Epicureans advocated a life of
withdrawal from larger society, such as the life led by Epicurus
himself with his students in his Garden.

   Epicurus thought that the anxiety human beings felt about
physical pain was less significant than the fear they had of the
gods and life after death. The Epicureans held that, though the
gods existed, they did not concern themselves with human
affairs. As the soul was mortal, fear of punishment after death
did not make sense. As Epicurus famously said, "Death is nothing to us." Religious anxiety, therefore, was unjustified. Thus, by
practicing temperance with respect to our natural desires and
having right beliefs about the gods and the soul, we could ensure
a tranquil life for ourselves. This good life required the virtues. As
I have already indicated with respect to temperance, the virtues
were necessary means to the end of tranquility. They may be very
closely related to that end, but their value was still *instrumental* to
achieving that final goal. This Epicurean view contrasts with that
of the Stoics, for whom the virtues are *intrinsic* to the good life,
*constitutive* of it. This is even true of practical wisdom or prudence,
which Epicurus regarded as "the greatest good ... even more
precious than philosophy ... [and] the natural source of all the
remaining virtues" (*Letter to Menoeceus*, 132). Epicurus thought
that it is impossible to live pleasantly without living prudently,
honorably, and justly, and impossible to live prudently, honorably,
and justly without living pleasantly. Prudence is what enables us
to choose those acts that are most productive of tranquility, and

to avoid those pleasures that lead, sooner or later, to an excess of pain. This was also true of friendship. Though Epicurus saw friendship as necessary for a good life, he saw its value as instrumental: friendship was justified because it enhanced the quality of one's own life.

Epicurus' conception of life is a minimalist one, involving withdrawal from public life, abandonment of any form of religious belief, beyond the beliefs that the gods exist and are happy, and abandonment of belief in the immortality of the soul. Epicurus' advice is: stop having anxiety about how things are going in your life; don't adopt goals other than the goal of attaining inner peace; gather around yourself a group of like-minded friends and enjoy life with them. Is this a philosophical life? We might ask the same question of the ideal of life recommended by the Stoics. Do the Epicurean and Stoic ideals of the good life involve philosophical activity? To some extent they do. An adherent to the Epicurean or Stoic philosophy would have to understand the principles of his or her chosen philosophy well enough to apply them in situations in daily life in order to reap the benefits of that philosophy. In another sense, however, they do not. Some members of the Epicurean or Stoic school, of course, might be engaged in a debate with representatives of rival schools over the relative merits of the schools' respective philosophies, such as that depicted in Cicero's dialogues. *That* activity would certainly be philosophical, and there is no question but that the leading proponents of Epicureanism and Stoicism, from Epicurus down to Marcus Aurelius, were philosophers. The life they recommended, however, though it might be philosophical in one sense, need not have been the life of someone we would identify as a philosopher.

Socrates' inquiries into virtue and the good life had a "ripple effect" on later philosophers. Plato and Aristotle, in somewhat different ways, offered answers to Socrates' questions. The Stoics rejected the complex moral psychology of Plato and Aristotle, and Aristotle's view that the best life required external goods. They returned to the Socratic view that virtue was knowledge. Even the Epicureans, who tried to distance themselves from this conversation to some extent, agreed that the point of ethics was to live the good life and that this required virtue. But this conversation raised other questions. If virtue was knowledge, then what was knowledge? If philosophy was care of the soul, then what was the soul? If virtue was harmony with nature, then what was nature? I'll turn to these questions in the following chapters.

# 2

# Knowledge and reality

*What is probable, gentlemen, is that in fact the god is wise, and that his oracular response meant that human wisdom is worth little or nothing, and that when he says this man, Socrates, he is using my name as an example, as if he said: "This man among you, mortals, is wisest who, like Socrates, understands that his wisdom is worthless."*

(Plato's *Apology*)

## Socrates

Socrates' statement is the result of a long process of discernment. Socrates describes in the *Apology* a question raised by his friend Chaerephon to the Delphic oracle, the most revered prophetic source among the Greeks. Chaerephon had asked the oracle whether anyone was wiser than Socrates. The oracle responded, "No one." Socrates was puzzled by the response, because he was not aware of being wise in any respect. He therefore undertook to examine the oracle's statement by trying to find an Athenian who was wise, thereby showing that the oracle was mistaken. He set out to examine the statesmen first, then the poets, and finally the artisans. His attempt failed. The political leaders of Athens turned out not to be wise at all, the poets (the "educators" of Greece) said wise things, but did not understand the meaning of what they said, and the skilled artisans thought that, because they had knowledge of their arts, they knew other things of greater importance, such as how to live or how to run a state. It turned out that the oracle was correct: Socrates was the wisest human being because he alone was aware of the extent of his own ignorance. This is human wisdom: to know what one does not know. (The Greek philosophers treated the terms "knowledge"—*epistêmê*—and wisdom—*sophia*—as equivalent.) Socrates does not exactly say, but he does suggest, that the gap between what the gods know (divine wisdom) and what we humans know is basically permanent.

What do the gods know? They know the nature of the virtues and the good life. After all, no one thinks the gods are unhappy: they lead blessed lives. (Socrates thought they lived morally perfect lives as well; this set him apart from the poets, who show the gods committing all sorts of immoral acts.) You will recall that Socrates thought that the basis of all ethical knowledge was knowledge of the definitions of the moral terms, in particular the virtues. He also put forward the view that virtue was nothing else but knowledge of this sort. As I said in chapter 1, Socrates was looking for conceptual knowledge, not knowledge of individual things. If the gods were wise, and if virtue was wisdom or knowledge, then the gods must have this knowledge. Socrates repeatedly uses the elenchus in Plato's dialogues to try to discover this definitional knowledge in others. He never succeeds. Therefore, it is reasonable to think that Socrates believed that the gods possessed this knowledge, but that humans lacked it, and were likely to continue to do so. In other words, there is a true ethical theory, replete with definitions of the key terms, which only the gods have, and probably will ever have. Human beings must be content with knowing that they don't possess this theory.

This distinction between divine and human wisdom is fundamental for all of the following accounts of knowledge offered by the philosophers we shall examine in this book. All of them attempt to answer the question "Can we have a kind of knowledge that is more than human, the kind that is possessed by the gods?" Socrates' answer to this question is *skeptical* in nature. Socrates doesn't deny the *existence* of a moral reality—he thinks there really is such a thing as the good life and the virtue that gives rise to it—he just doubts that we humans can *know* that reality. And yet … later in the *Apology* Socrates declares that he has *some* moral knowledge. He knows, he says, that it is always wrong to disobey a superior. How can he claim to know this, especially if all knowledge depends on definitions and Socrates denies that he has definitional knowledge of the virtues? This tension between his general profession of ignorance and his particular claims to know some moral truth is part of the paradox that is Socrates. I don't think it has an answer.

Most interpreters have found Socrates' professions of ignorance difficult to accept at face value. Most would be uncomfortable with my claim that Socrates is a moral skeptic. It has been suggested that, though Socrates may not have knowledge in the strictest sense of the term, perhaps he has knowledge in some weaker sense. Perhaps when he denies that he has knowledge he is speaking in that strict, philosophical sense, but when he says that he knows that disobedience to a superior is wrong he is speaking less strictly, perhaps colloquially. Perhaps the term "knowledge" is ambiguous. This raises a question, however: if there *is* a strict philosophical sense of the word "knowledge," what is it? The branch of philosophy that studies the nature of knowledge and attempts to determine the conditions under which knowledge claims can be justified is called "epistemology," from *epistêmê*, "knowledge," and *logos*, a "rational account." Epistemology is thus the branch of philosophy that offers a rational account of knowledge. In one sense of the term, Socrates is not an epistemologist. He doesn't—at least not in the Platonic dialogues most scholars regard as Socratic—ask, "What is knowledge?" He doesn't set out a list of necessary and sufficient conditions for knowledge. On the other hand, he talks about knowledge all the time: he denies that he has knowledge, he identifies virtue with knowledge, he examines others to see if they have knowledge, and so on. In a dialogue that starts out like a typical Socratic dialogue, the *Meno*, Socrates *does* offer an account of the nature of knowledge and distinguishes it from true belief. In another dialogue, the *Theaetetus*, the most sustained discussion of knowledge in the Platonic corpus, Socrates gives a critique of three concepts of knowledge: first, that knowledge is perception; second, that knowledge is true belief; and third, that knowledge is true belief plus an account. This last definition is the one he had reached in the *Meno*. Most interpreters believe that these discussions of knowledge in the *Meno* and *Theaetetus* really represent *Plato's* thought rather than that of Socrates, and that is the interpretation I'll follow in this chapter. Still, as in other cases, it is hard to know where Socrates ends and where Plato begins. So what does he mean when he makes these claims and asks these questions?

First of all, when Socrates talks about knowledge, he is talking about a mental state, a state of some individual person, like other states such as belief and ignorance. We might of course speak in some contexts of knowledge as a subject area, a "body of knowledge" such as for instance "mathematical knowledge," without worrying about whether anyone possessed that knowledge, but, when Socrates worries about whether there is any such thing as ethical knowledge, he is worrying about whether anyone, apart from the gods, is in such a mental state. Second, knowledge is not *simply* a mental state; it is, like belief and ignorance, a mental state that is related to reality, to truth. It is a *cognitive* mental state. If I know the definition of piety or justice, that definition must describe, accurately, some feature of the world. There must be a *correspondence* of some sort between my definition and reality. Only then will my definition be *true*.

When we say that I *know* some fact or other, I am saying more than that the statement that expresses that fact is true. Let's assume for the moment that I am saying, in addition, that I *believe* this statement. (Plato talks about knowledge and belief in the *Republic* as if they were exclusive of each other, but most people, and in fact Plato in most of his dialogues, think that knowledge involves belief.) But when I say I *know* some statement to be true I am claiming more than that I *believe* the statement and that it is true. (I may believe that I left the water running in the bathroom, but I may not know that for a fact until I go and check.) What is the difference between knowledge and true belief? Plato in the *Meno* has Socrates say that knowledge involves a rational explanation of what I believe. He criticizes this definition of knowledge at the end of the *Theaetetus*, but this definition—that knowledge is true belief plus a rational account, *justified* true belief—has proved to be the most influential definition of knowledge in the history of philosophy. Philosophers have had a good deal of trouble over the years explaining what counts as an adequate justification, but they have generally thought that something like this account must be correct.

What counts as an adequate justification? Let's suppose that it is one that excludes doubt. If I want to know whether I left the water on in the bathroom, I can simply check. Practically, that will settle things. But for some philosophers, that might not be sufficient. Perhaps I can't rely on my senses for some reason, such as that I may be actually asleep and dreaming that I left the water on. Perhaps there is some other reason why my ordinary justification procedures won't work in this particular situation; or worse, why they don't work adequately in general. Then I might require a higher standard of justification for knowledge. The highest standard of justification, I suppose, is *proof*, such as one finds in mathematics. Suppose that, as philosophers, we insist that knowledge must measure up to this standard. Now we are dealing with knowledge in a strict sense of the term. Suppose philosophical knowledge does not merely exclude actual doubt, but that it excludes the very *possibility* of doubt. Suppose strict philosophical knowledge has to be *infallible*, certain. We can then understand philosophical knowledge as the infallible cognition of truth, or of reality.

This is the conception of knowledge that Plato shows Socrates employing in his Socratic dialogues. It is, I believe, the *only* conception of knowledge that Socrates has. His standards for ethical knowledge are very high; that is part of the reason why none of his interlocutors ever satisfies them. We can see just how high the threshold for knowledge is for Socrates by looking at one of his remarks in the *Gorgias*, which I mentioned in chapter 1. After having presented his most powerful objections to Callicles' view that the best life for a human being is a life of pleasure and of dominance over others, Socrates says that his conclusions are "bound by arguments of iron and adamant"; yet he goes on to say, "I don't know how these things are." What more could one ask for than "arguments of iron and adamant?" What more would it take to convert such conclusions into knowledge? Perhaps Socrates is just offering his usual disclaimer of knowledge here, and perhaps he doesn't really mean it; but I would think that if he had some weaker conception of knowledge available he might have stated it at this point. He might have said, in particular, "my conclusions are bound by arguments of iron and adamant, and that is why I claim to know them." But this is not what he says. I suspect that what is behind Socrates' disclaimer in the *Gorgias* is the conclusion of the *Apology* that only the god is wise. However strong his arguments might be, they must inevitably fall short of that divine standard, and thus of knowledge in the strict sense. Could anyone know what a god knows? For the gods' knowledge, not just of ethics but of all things, is essentially perfect and complete, at least as Socrates understands it.

Skepticism comes in several varieties and degrees. One could be a skeptic about knowledge of the external world, or about the existence of other minds, or about the existence of God or the gods, to mention only three possibilities. Socrates' skepticism is limited to ethics, and perhaps to the first principles of ethics. To list four degrees of skepticism from the weakest to the strongest:

1) One could *doubt* whether anyone *actually has* knowledge.
2) One could *deny* that anyone *actually has* knowledge.
3) One could *doubt* whether knowledge is even *possible*.
4) One could *deny* that knowledge is even *possible*.

Socrates is a skeptic of at least the weakest sort; he may hold to a stronger version of skepticism, depending on how we interpret his comment that only the god is wise. His skeptical stance in the *Apology* does not rule out searching for moral truth: he clearly does that throughout Plato's Socratic dialogues. He even seems to make progress in defining the moral properties he is searching for; at times, as at the end of the *Euthyphro*, he seems almost to have reached his goal. Yet the goal remains tantalizingly out of reach: not once in Plato's Socratic dialogues is a satisfactory definition of a moral virtue reached. (Xenophon, our other source of information about Socrates, is much more optimistic about the possibility of definition than Plato. In his *Memorabilia*—IV.6, he offers a raft of definitions, beginning with a definition of piety. It may be that Xenophon was aiming to correct Plato's view of Socrates, which he may have regarded as excessively skeptical.) As I indicated in chapter 1, this produces a paradox, perhaps the ultimate paradox of Socrates: he claimed that virtue is knowledge, he denied that he had any such knowledge, and yet he seemed to those who knew him the most virtuous person, the "best, and also the wisest and the most upright" of his age.

# Plato

Different philosophers found different ways of dealing with this paradox. The skeptical Socrates became the model of philosophical activity in the Academy in the third and second centuries BCE, when Arcesilaus and Carneades denied the possibility of knowledge in their debates with the Stoics. The Stoics, on the other hand, took Socrates as perhaps the only viable historical model of the sage, and, since they attributed infallibility to the sage, they had to discount Socrates' professions of ignorance. Plato took a middle path: while continuing to adhere to the picture of Socrates as an ignorant inquirer, he turned him into a philosopher with a positive, constructive view of knowledge. (From here on, I'll be talking mainly about Plato's views, though the character in the dialogues who expresses them remains Socrates.) Actually, he shows us two solutions to the paradox: he offers two positive accounts of knowledge. One we have already seen, in chapter 1: the philosopher climbs out of the cave and obtains knowledge of the Good. The other occurs in the *Meno*, at a point where Socrates' examination of Meno has broken down, in a manner typical of the Socratic dialogues. Meno has tried several times to define virtue, and is frustrated when his latest attempt fails, just as the others have. How will you look for virtue if you do not know what it is? he asks Socrates. Even if you find it, how will you recognize it as what you are seeking? Plato's answer is the *doctrine of recollection*:

1) The soul is immortal and has been endlessly reincarnated.
2) It has learned all things in its previous lives.
3) It can now, under the proper circumstances, recollect what it had previously learned.
4) As "all nature is akin," once it has recalled one thing, it may be able to recollect all the rest.
5) What is called "learning," therefore, is actually recollection.

Socrates illustrates the doctrine of recollection by examining a slave-boy from Meno's retinue on a geometrical construction.

Like Meno, the slave-boy is initially unable to state the correct answer, but under Socratic questioning he finally does so, on the third try. At that point in the recollective process, says Socrates, the slave-boy has only true belief, not knowledge; the beliefs have a dream-like quality to them. But if he is examined in many ways on the same point he will eventually have a knowledge as exact as anyone's. The slave-boy example is important because it shows how recollection works in the case of clear-cut, established knowledge of the highest certainty: mathematics. The suggestion, which I believe Plato takes seriously, is that ethics can be as precise as geometry if only we can begin with the right definitions of terms.

There are several questions that might be raised about the doctrine of recollection. The first is: where does the idea that the soul is immortal and endlessly reincarnated come from? I'll deal with that issue in chapter 3. Another question is: if knowledge is in our souls when we are born, why is it not active at once? Plato gives an imaginative, mythical answer to this question. Souls about to be born drink from the River *Lêthê*, which causes them to "forget" their knowledge, to lose active awareness of it. Nonetheless, it remains latent in their souls, ready to be recovered under proper stimuli. A third question might be: isn't this theory rather extravagant? Isn't it like using a howitzer to kill a fly? In answer, Plato might say that the problem of knowledge is a very serious one in epistemology, not at all like killing a fly. Other philosophers in later years made use of concepts like innate ideas, categories of understanding, and the language of thought to explain the possibility of knowledge. The contemporary linguist Noam Chomsky at various points in his career proposed different answers to the question "How is it that a young child of three years can construct complex sentences he or she has never heard before?" Chomsky called this "Plato's problem," and he had this passage in mind in doing so. He took it very seriously.

The conclusion of Socrates' argument is that all learning is recollection. Actually, this conclusion is overstated. There must be two stages in the recollection process. Stage one, the initial learning, is not a matter of recollection but of direct acquaintance. Stage two, which only occurs when the knowledge possessed in stage one has been forgotten, is the recollection of what was previously directly known. Second, the slave-boy example gives us a distinction between knowledge and true belief. At the end of the *Meno*, Socrates returns to this topic. Socrates and Meno had agreed that virtue was knowledge, but they were perplexed because there were no teachers of virtue. (Socrates, the obvious example of a teacher of virtue, recuses himself on the grounds that he has no knowledge.) Socrates proposes that right belief or opinion can be as good a practical guide to virtue as knowledge, for as long as one has it. The problem with right opinion is that, unlike knowledge, it is not stable. It escapes just when you want it. But right opinion can be converted to knowledge by proper questioning, by the elenchus, which tethers the opinion by a rational argument. Socrates says that one of the very few things that he would claim to *know* is that knowledge and right opinion are different.

Socrates does not say in the *Meno* exactly what kind of knowledge is recollected. In another dialogue, the *Phaedo*, which was presumably written after the *Meno*, he does. The objects of knowledge that we recollect are *Forms*. Plato actually introduces the concept of Form in the *Euthyphro*, a Socratic dialogue. In two passages, Socrates asks his interlocutor Euthyphro to explain what piety is in general, not just in some particular instance: he asks,

> is the pious not the same and alike in every action, and the impious the opposite of all that is pious and like itself, and [does not] everything that is to be impious present us with one Form ... in so far as it is impious?"

> (*Euthyphr.* 5d; my addition in brackets)

When Euthyphro fails to understand Socrates' question, he repeats it:

> I did not bid you tell me one or two of the many pious actions, but that Form itself that makes all pious actions pious; for you agreed that all impious actions are impious and all pious actions pious through one Form, or don't you remember? ... Tell me then, what this Form is, so that I may look upon it, and using it as a model, say that any action of yours or another's that is of that kind is pious, and if it is not that it is not.
>
> *(Euthyphr.* 6d–e; I capitalize "Form")

In these two passages, Plato uses three terms to characterize what he is looking for: *eidos*, *idea*, and *paradeigma*; the first two of these are terms for "Form"; the last means "model" or "standard" (literally, "paradigm"). He will use these repeatedly over the course of his career to refer to Forms.

What is a Form? First of all, it is the objective, the goal, of Socratic inquiry; it is what Socrates was trying to define. Socrates was seeking what philosophers call a "real" definition; a definition not just of a term (that would be a "nominal" definition) but of the thing associated with the term. Second, it is the referent of a general term: "piety," "justice," "courage," and the like refer to Forms. We might divide terms into two sorts: there are particular terms, such as "Socrates," which refer to particular things or individual persons. Then there are general terms, such as "pious," "just," courageous," as well as "red," "square," "two feet tall," and countless others. General terms are *predicated of* individuals: we say that Socrates was just and that Secretariat was fast. Conceptual knowledge is knowledge of the meaning of these general terms. To what, if anything, do these general terms refer? Over the centuries, philosophers have given several answers to this question. Here are three that have been especially influential:

1) "Pious" refers to the property of piety, which characterizes multiple individuals, such as Socrates. Such a property is a real component of things. It is a *universal*. (Realism)
2) "Pious" refers to the concept of piety, a mental entity. It is a component of our conceptual scheme and has no reality outside that scheme. Universals exist only in our minds. (Conceptualism)
3) "Pious" does not refer to anything. It is a linguistic entity, a word we use to describe things. Piety is not something real over and above Socrates and other pious individuals. Universals do not exist, either in the mind or in reality. (Nominalism)

The Socrates of the *Euthyphro* is a metaphysical realist. He believes in universals that exist outside the mind, at least one of which is Piety. (I use the capital "P" to indicate that this is the name of a Form.) This is the first step in the development of Plato's theory of Forms: the claim that, in addition to particulars, there exist universals. This is the step that occurs in the passages of the *Euthyphro* quoted above. It also occurs in some other Socratic dialogues, such as the *Protagoras* and *Hippias Major*. Though some philosophers (nominalists) object to the claim that universal properties exist, and that general terms refer to them, it is not very controversial in itself—it is almost a matter of common sense—and most of Socrates' interlocutors in Plato's Socratic dialogues accept it without thinking much about it. One might even object to calling this a philosophical theory, on the ground that the claim that there is "something" in the world answering to the word "piety" is trivially true. The second step is much more controversial. It consists in three additional claims:

1) That the Forms have a mode of existence *separate from* the particulars that participate in them.

2) That they are the only true objects of knowledge.
3) That they are "more real" than the particulars that share in them.

How did Plato come to add these very controversial claims to what otherwise could have been seen as a commonsense view of properties? Aristotle offers an answer in his discussion of the views of his predecessors in Book I of his *Metaphysics*. In chapter 6, discussing the views of Plato, he writes that in his youth Plato had become familiar, through a certain Cratylus, with the views of the Presocratic philosopher Heraclitus, who held that all sensible things were in a state of perpetual flux, and that therefore there was no knowledge of them. Aristotle says that Plato accepted Socrates' view that the objects of definition were universals, but he held that the definitions could not apply to sensible things, because they were always changing. Therefore, the definitions had to apply to Forms that existed apart from sensible things. Plato does not confirm this Aristotelian account in so many words in any one place in his dialogues, but he does say things in various places that support Aristotle's account. In the *Theaetetus*, he shows that, in a Heraclitean world of perpetual flux, there could be no knowledge. In the *Phaedo*, a dialogue linked to the *Meno* by reference to the doctrine of recollection, he argues that the equal things we see, such as sticks and stones, only imperfectly instantiate perfect Equality. Since we never experience perfect Equality while using our senses—that is, while we are living on earth—we must have experienced it before we were born and recollected it later. Thus, perfect Equality, a Form, cannot exist in the sensible world. In the *Symposium*, he says that the ultimate Beauty is always in existence—it does not come to be or pass away—and it is not beautiful in one respect but not in another, or at one time but not another, or in relation to one thing but not another, or in the opinion of some people but not others, and so on. It is simply beautiful, without qualification, and it exists "itself by itself with itself." All the many beautiful things,

the things we see around us, however, are only relatively beautiful. They "participate in" the Form of Beauty, but they are not
identical to it. Rather, they imitate, or imperfectly resemble, the
Form itself, which is a model, a paradigm, as Socrates had already
said in the *Euthyphro*.

This view that there are two kinds of thing—intelligible, eternal
Forms and sensible, temporally limited particulars—is developed
most fully in the central books of the *Republic*, in particular Book V.
In this book of the *Republic*, Plato deals with a number of objections to the account of justice he has developed in Books II–IV. The
most serious objection, in his view, is that the ideally just state never
could come into being. To this objection, Plato has two answers.
The first is that the objective of the previous discussion had been
to develop a model, a paradigm, in order to understand justice. As it
would be no criticism of a painter who painted an ideally beautiful human being if it turned out that no actual human being ever
perfectly resembled the painting, so it is no criticism of the model
that they have developed if it turns out that no state perfectly
exemplifies that model. It would be enough if a state could come
close to the perfection of the model. His second answer is based
on the first. It is that a close approximation of the model could be
created if philosophers became kings, or if kings became philosophers. Glaucon's response is that this claim would be greeted with
general derision, or worse: people would take up arms if they heard
Socrates say such a thing.

Plato's response to Glaucon's objection is to distinguish
between two sorts of person: the philosopher and the "lover of
sights and sounds." He does so by first distinguishing the Beautiful itself, the Form of Beauty, from the many beautiful things.
Lovers of sights and sounds love the many beautiful things, but
they do not love the Beautiful itself; they don't even acknowledge its existence. The philosopher, on the other hand, knows the
Beautiful itself. The lovers of sights and sounds spend their time
discussing the relative merits of this play or that, this sculpture or

that, this painting or that, but their discussion can't yield knowledge because they don't understand the nature of Beauty itself. They can express opinions, but they don't have knowledge. The philosopher, on the other hand, knows what absolute Beauty is, and can see how the many beautiful things of this world approximate to it, but do not equal it. The philosopher has knowledge, while the lover of sights and sounds has only opinion; the former is awake, the latter only dreaming. The Forms, being completely knowable, are completely real; the many beautiful things, on the other hand, are only imperfectly real. They exist, but only for a time; they participate in beauty, but imperfectly, relatively.

In *Republic* V, Plato backtracks on the account of knowledge and right opinion he gave at the end of the *Meno*. There he had said that opinion and knowledge had the same objects, but that opinion was converted to knowledge by the addition of a rational account. Now he says that knowledge and opinion are different powers; knowledge is infallible, whereas opinion is fallible; knowledge is of the completely real, whereas opinion is of the imperfectly real, what hovers between being and not-being. There are thus two "worlds" for Plato: a world of knowledge, consisting of the Forms, and a world of opinion, consisting of sensible things. Plato called the first the world of Being and the second the world of Becoming. The link between them is the relation of participation: sensible things participate in Forms, and derive their properties from that fact.

Forms are primarily eternal objects of knowledge, exempted from the perpetual change of the sensible world and placed in an intelligible world of their own. Properties result from the participation of sensible particulars in the Forms. Participation is the relation that grounds predication for Plato: to say that Socrates is pious is to say that Socrates participates in Piety. But what is participation? Aristotle says Plato left this an open question. Plato's clearest account seems to be that participation is imitation: that Forms are paradigms—models, standards, or patterns—that sensible particulars imitate, but Aristotle dismisses this account as "empty words and poetic metaphors."

For the moment, however, let us leave aside the problem of participation. Plato's theory of Forms is a *metaphysical* theory—an account of the ultimate principles of the universe. More specifically, it is an *ontology*: an account of what exists. This metaphysical, ontological theory is, however, intimately related to Plato's theory of knowledge, his epistemology. Plato, unlike Socrates, *does* attempt to explain what knowledge is and how we acquire it. Plato has the same high standards for knowledge that Socrates had, or perhaps even higher: he is concerned with knowledge in the strict, philosophical sense. For both Socrates and Plato, knowledge is inherently general, universal. It would not be correct, according to Plato, to say that I had knowledge, *epistêmê*, of some particular fact, such as where my car keys are. (If that sounds strange, remember that "knowledge" was equivalent to "wisdom." *Epistêmê* is also often translated "science," especially by translators of Aristotle. There is no *wisdom* whose object is the location of my car keys. There is no *science* of the location of my keys either, however much I might wish at times that there were.) The kind of knowledge that Socrates was looking for, as I said in the last chapter, is *conceptual*, not *perceptual*. According to Plato, knowledge—genuine knowledge as opposed to opinion—is awareness, understanding, of the Forms. As I mentioned above, Plato offers two accounts of how we acquire this knowledge. One is that we recollect what we knew prior to our current earthly lives. The other is that we can climb out of the cave while we are alive and ascend to the world of the Forms and, ultimately, the Good. Both accounts rely on the idea that we have, at some point, direct awareness of these Forms. In the *Symposium*, he describes such an ascent of the lover from love of a single beautiful human body through various stages of love to the ultimate experience of Beauty itself. In the account of Forms in the *Euthyphro*, in which Forms are common properties of things around us, this direct awareness should be commonplace, though no one Socrates examines proves to have knowledge of what these Forms are. In Plato's version of the theory of Forms, knowledge of the Forms is extremely rare. It can only be reached, Plato says in the *Republic*, after ten years of education in mathematics, followed by five more years of education in "dialectic"—that is, philosophy.

Plato clearly thought that knowledge in the strict, philosophical sense was possible. He bases his claim that philosophers should rule in the ideal state on their possession of knowledge of the Form of the Good. But he does not cite any actual person who had the kind of direct experience of the Forms that he attributes to the philosopher–king. He does not say that Socrates had it. (If Socrates did have it, then his skepticism, his profession of ignorance, would be an ironic pose. Alcibiades actually suggests this in the *Symposium*, but Socrates never admits that he has knowledge of the Forms.) Plato does not say that he himself had it. Thus, his response to the skepticism of Socrates is somewhat hypothetical: knowledge is possible, and indeed it is necessary if philosophers are to be kings, but it is the result of a difficult and arduous process. Ultimately, the kind of knowledge Plato attributes to the philosophers is complete understanding of the entire system of Forms. It is the kind of knowledge Socrates says in the *Apology* that only the god possesses. Plato offers a picture of the attainment of this knowledge in the *Phaedrus*: he describes a procession of gods around the circumference of the universe, in which they gaze steadily at the Forms. Human souls join this procession and catch glimpses of the Forms; but, weighed down by earthly desires, they cannot sustain the vision of the gods and fall to earth. This passage combines the idea of recollection with that of direct experience. In some sense, it unifies Plato's two accounts of knowledge. The philosopher's soul, encountering earthly beauty, "grows wings" and ascends to the world of the Forms; other souls remain earthbound.

Plato, unlike Socrates, is thus not a skeptic. He does not deny that a human being might have the knowledge of a god.

In fact, he insists that we can, and provides an account of how we might obtain such knowledge. A part of Socrates' skepticism remains in Plato's view, however, in the claim that knowledge is an ideal that only the philosopher can attain, and in the fact that he cannot name any actual individual who has attained this ultimate stage of complete knowledge. Knowledge in the strict philosophical sense is possible, but not actual. It is an ideal. This "two worlds" picture of knowledge and reality actually contains a problem, which Plato raises in the *Parmenides*. In this dialogue, Plato depicts a very young Socrates in conversation with Parmenides, a Presocratic philosopher Plato greatly admired. Socrates puts forward the theory of Forms, as I have described it above, as an answer to a paradox devised by Parmenides' disciple Zeno. Parmenides raises a number of objections to the theory, the last of which is this: if the gods live in their world, the world of the Forms, the world of "Knowledge," while we live in our world and have only "knowledge," an imitation of the Form of Knowledge, of particular things, then how can we ever bridge the gap between the two worlds? Parmenides says that this is the greatest difficulty faced by someone who posits the existence of a separately existing world of Forms. Difficulties such as this lead people to doubt that separate Forms exist, but he indicates that they can be answered, though only by a very gifted person; and it would require someone of even greater gifts to teach another the solutions to these problems. On the other hand, if one does not posit Forms, one will have nothing to fix one's thought on, and that will destroy what Parmenides calls the power of dialectic. (The Greek word *dialegesthai* could mean "conversation"; Parmenides may be saying that without Forms there not only could be no philosophy, but no speech.) The theory of Forms is not only an answer to the questions "What exists?" and "What can I know?"; it is also an answer to the question "What is the meaning of words such as "'good,' 'beautiful,' and the like?" It is a semantic theory as well as an ontology and epistemology.

Plato thus gives us a clear indication, through the words of Parmenides, that the "greatest difficulty" facing the Forms, and other problems he mentions, can be solved. He does not think these objections are by any means fatal to the theory. On the other hand, he does not tell us anywhere what the solutions to these problems are. This has led some interpreters to think that Plato modified, or even abandoned, the theory of Forms in response to the critique of the *Parmenides*. There are several passages in dialogues written either around the same time as or after the *Parmenides* that indicate that he retained the theory, but he may have developed it further. In the middle of the *Theaetetus*, in a passage labeled a digression, in which Plato describes the difference between the lawyer and the philosopher in ways that strongly recall the *Gorgias*, he says that "two patterns (paradigms, models) are set up in reality. One is divine and supremely happy; the other has nothing of God in it and is the pattern of the deepest unhappiness" (*Tht.* 176e). Clearly, these correspond to the philosophical life and the life of the lawyer. The philosophical life is godlike, and Plato says that one must attempt to escape the evils of life on earth and become as much like God as possible. This happens when one becomes "just and pure, with understanding." "Becoming like God" becomes the goal of ethics for Plato in his later works. In the *Philebus*, Plato describes a method, which he identifies as dialectic and which he describes as "collection and division," whereby one can collect the many instances of "man" or "ox," "beautiful" and "good" into a single unit and divide this unit again into several kinds. In the *Sophist*, he describes the relations between what he calls five of the "greatest kinds" (he also refers to them as "Forms")—Being, Sameness, Difference, Rest, and Motion—arguing that these Forms all "blend" with each other in specific ways. In the *Timaeus*, he states succinctly that, if knowledge differs from belief, then Forms must exist as objects of knowledge. In the *Seventh Letter*, the author (who may or may not be Plato) mentions five things that must be distinguished if a Form is to be known: the name, the definition, the image, knowledge, and finally "the object itself, the knowable and truly real being." So it looks as though Plato never abandoned his commitment to Forms, though he articulated it by explaining how Forms "blend" and divide in various ways. (Aristotle gives us no indication that Plato ever abandoned the theory of separately existing Forms or its corresponding epistemology either, though he does indicate that Plato late in life came to identify Forms with numbers.)

# Aristotle

Plato's metaphysics and epistemology are answers to the problem of divine and human wisdom raised by Socrates. They show how it is possible for a human being to ascend to the world of the Forms or, alternatively, to recollect what he or she had known before birth. They are not skeptical theories; however, because Plato is unable to name anyone who has attained the knowledge he describes, they do retain an element of Socrates' skepticism. They also come at a high cost: the positing of a separate world for the Forms and the problem of participation. Aristotle wanted to retain the advantages of Plato's system without its high costs. When thinking of Aristotle's account of knowledge and reality, there are basically three things to note. First, he was a member of Plato's Academy for twenty years. Plato's influence on him is deep, though he is quite critical of Plato. Second, he was a great biologist. Third, he was a great logician. These three aspects of his thought combine to produce Aristotle's answer to the questions "What is real?" and "What can I know?" Stylistically, Aristotle is worlds apart from Plato. If Plato is the poet of classical metaphysics and epistemology, Aristotle is the natural scientist. Though there is plenty of dialectic in Aristotle, in general, he is dogmatic where Plato is dialectical.

What Aristotle objected to in Plato's view of reality was the positing of two worlds: the separation of the world of Being—the world of eternal, intelligible Forms—from the world of Becoming, the sensible world. Aristotle wanted only a single world, in which the Forms were integrated with sensible reality. He thought that Socrates was right not to separate the Forms; he wanted to go back to Socrates' view, but seen from a biological perspective. He had a battery of specific objections to Plato's theory, but he wanted to retain the concept of "form" without Plato's separate Forms. He knew from his biological works that animals come in kinds, and that most of the time they "breed true." In general, reproduction is the transmission of the specific form of an animal of a particular species to another member of the same species. One of his most frequent statements of this fact is: "Man begets man." His metaphysics, philosophy of nature ("physics"), and biology are all developed with that fact in mind. The centrality of form in Aristotle's thought is one of the things that link Socrates, Plato and Aristotle, and that makes them, in spite of their differences, part of a single, continuous conversation.

One of the two fundamental concepts in Aristotle's philosophy (along with that of form) is *substance*. The concept of substance has its roots in his logical writings, and in particular in his *Categories*. The *Categories* deals with general terms which are predicated of individuals. According to Aristotle, there are ten categories: substance, quality, quantity, relation, place, time, position, state, action, and affection (see figure 1). "Is a horse" is a predicate in the category of substance; "is red" is a predicate in the category of quality; "is six feet tall" is a predicate in the category of "quantity," and so on. These constitute the basic kinds of things that can be asserted, predicated, of something. To each of these linguistic items, there corresponds a kind of thing in the world: to "horse" corresponds the natural kind horse; to "red" corresponds the color red, and so on. I'll refer to entities in all of these categories as "attributes." Thus, the *Categories* is both a

**Figure 1:** Aristotle's categories

| | Substance | Quality | Quantity | Other Categories |
|---|---|---|---|---|
| *Secondary* | Animal | Color | Height | General attribute (e.g. location) |
| | Human being, horse | Pale (white), roan (red) | Five feet, six feet, etc. | Specific attribute (e.g. in the Lyceum) |
| *Primary* | Socrates, Secretariat | Socrates' pallor, Secretariat's roan color | Socrates' height, Secretariat's height | Location of Socrates, Location of Secretariat |

classification of linguistic items and of their corresponding attributes. It is both a work of grammar, answering the question "What are the terms of a sentence, or proposition?" and a work of ontology, answering the question "Of what is the world made?" Our statements, and in particular those that attribute something to individuals, have a structure parallel to that of the world. Aristotle adheres to a *correspondence theory of truth*: a statement is true if there is a state of affairs in the world to which it corresponds. To use the cliché example, "The cat is on the mat" is true if and only if the cat is on the mat.

So far, I have been talking about predicates, general terms, and their corresponding attributes. These predicates, however, all must ultimately be predicates of something that is not itself a predicate, but a subject, an individual substance; something that can be referred to by a proper name, such as "Socrates" or "Secretariat," or, if it does not have a proper name, by a phrase such as "this tree" or "that squirrel." Ultimately, the simplest kind of statement is one made up of a subject term, naming an individual substance, and a predicate term—for example, "Socrates is a human being," "Secretariat is red," "This tree is six feet tall," or "That squirrel is in the tree." Now it is possible to have subject–predicate sentences that do not refer to individual substances, such as "Red is a color" or "The horse is an animal," but Aristotle thinks that the truth of sentences of this kind depends ultimately on whether they are grounded in predications of individual substances. For Plato, "The horse is an animal" is a statement about the Form of Horse and its relation to the Form of Animal. It would be true whether or not there are individual horses, such as Secretariat. For Aristotle, that is not the case. Aristotle thinks that, if there were no individual horses, then the universal, horse, would not exist. For Aristotle, the existence of universals depends on the existence of the appropriate individuals. Aristotle reverses the priority between universals and particulars that Plato had defended: for Aristotle, unlike Plato, it is the particular, not the universal, that is ultimate. To put the matter in the language of Plato's metaphysics, for Plato the individual horse, Secretariat, is but an imitation, a copy, a sensible instance, of the Form of Horse. Aristotle doesn't use the language of imitation (recall that he said this way of speaking was a poetic metaphor), but Plato, looking at Aristotle's metaphysics, would say that Aristotle had made the universal a pale shadow of the particular. The universal is real, for Aristotle, but in a secondary sense. This is what interpreters have meant by calling Aristotle a *moderate*, and Plato an *extreme* realist.

The ontology of the *Categories* is one that describes the individual substance as fundamental, as the most basic kind of thing there is. It suggests that, as Secretariat and Socrates are primary substances, they are simple, not analyzable into something more basic. In the *Physics*, however, Aristotle divides the individual substance of the *Categories* into two parts: matter and form. In *Physics* II.3, Aristotle distinguishes four "causes" or "explanatory principles" of a thing: matter, form, the moving cause, and the final cause. Each individual thing is composed of matter and form: the matter is that out of which a thing is made and the form is the organizing principle that turns the matter into a finished product. The moving cause of something's coming to be is what is responsible for the thing's existence or what makes it what it is: e.g. the father in the case of the child. (Aristotle believed that in reproduction the male parent transmitted its form to the offspring, while the female parent contributed the matter.) The final cause is the purpose served by what comes to be. In order to see how the causes work, let me make a distinction between natural substances and artifacts. Artifacts are, simply, things built by artisans: beds, tables, statues, and the like. They require an external agent if they are to exist: without the artisan, the matter will never become a product. Natural substances, on the other hand, have their productive principle within themselves. It is for this reason that Aristotle regards them as the only true substances. Human beings reproduce by nature, and infant humans grow up in time to be fully grown, fully functional humans. In the case of artifacts, the four causes are distinct: the bronze is the matter out of which the statue is made, the shape of the statue is its form, the sculptor is the moving cause, and the purpose served by the statue, perhaps the honoring of a great leader, is the final cause. Or think of a house: the matter is the wood, brick, tiles, etc., out of which the house is made. The form is the plan or blueprint according to which the house is built, or, as Aristotle says, the idea in the mind of the builder. The moving cause is the builder of the house, and the final cause, the purpose of the house, is to provide habitation for people. In the case of natural objects, however, the formal, efficient, and final causes tend to coincide: the cause of the existence of a human being is another human being, what comes to be is a human being, and that for the sake of which it comes to be is a human being. That is, the point of creating a human being is simply to have a fully functioning human being. Thus, it would seem that the basic distinction Aristotle is attempting to draw with regard to natural substances is between matter and form.

Of these two causes, matter and form, the primary cause is the form. The form, rather than the matter, explains the nature of a thing. The primary explanatory principle of nature, in fact, is form. This view of the composition of an individual substance is known as *hylomorphism*, from *hylê*, meaning "matter," and *morphê*, meaning "form." Closely related to the distinction between matter and form is another distinction, between *potentiality* and *actuality*. The matter of a thing explains what it *can be*, its potentiality; the form, what it *is*, its actuality. Aristotle's terms for potentiality and actuality are *dunamis*, from which we get the term "dynamic," and *energeia*, from which we get "energy." Aristotle associates potentiality with matter, actuality with form. Several pieces of lumber, of the right shape and size, may potentially be a bed, or a table. When assembled, they take on the form of a bed or table and become an actual bed or table. The lumber is *potentially* a bed, but

it is also *actually* lumber. In general, things cannot be potentially
X unless they are actually Y. Aristotle thinks that the concrete
natural substances that make up our world are combinations of
matter and form, potentiality and actuality. Consider, for example,
a human being. If one analyzes a human being completely, down
to its most basic components, Aristotle thinks, one will find that
it is made of the opposites: hot and cold, wet and dry. But if you
ask what a human being is made of, it would be wrong to say,
"hot and cold, wet and dry." Rather, the opposites combine to
form elements: fire, air, water, and earth. These elements in turn
combine to form various kinds of stuff out of which the bodily
organs are made: bone, sinew, muscle, gut, and so forth. These
parts in their turn form the organs themselves: the clavicle, the
gluteus maximus, the large intestine, the heart, etc. These organs
in turn combine to form systems: the skeletal system, the muscu-
lar system, the digestive system, the circulatory system, the nerv-
ous system, and the like. (I use modern terminology; Aristotle was
not aware that blood circulated, and he thought the brain was an
organ for cooling the blood.) These systems, finally, combine to
form a human body. Each stage of development is matter for the
next, more complex stage; it is *potentially* what that next stage is
*actually*. The final potentiality/actuality pair is the fully articulated
human body and the human being: the body is matter for the
human form, potentiality for the actuality of the human being.

Now, however, a problem arises. In the *Categories*, it was
clear that the individual substance, Secretariat or Socrates, was
the primary substance, the primary kind of thing that exists. In
the *Physics*, however, the primary substance of the *Categories* was
analyzed further, into matter and form. Now is one of these two,
matter or form, primary substance, or does the individual retain
its status? Aristotle investigates this question in the central books
of the *Metaphysics*, his deepest discussion of substance. It is an
extremely complex discussion: scholars have long debated what
Aristotle's doctrine of substance in these books is. On the one

hand, Aristotle says that a substance must be a "this," an individual. This suggests that the individual human being or horse, Socrates or Secretariat, retains the role of primary substance it had in the *Categories*. On the other, he seems to dismiss the claims of the concrete individual to be primary, on the grounds that such beings have a composite nature. What is primary about Socrates is clearly his form, rather than his matter, which suggests that form is primary substance. But the form of Socrates is simply the species man, *homo sapiens*, and this is a universal. It has often been said that Aristotle is committed to an inconsistent triad of propositions:

1) Primary substance is form.
2) Form is universal.
3) No universal is a substance.

It looks in the end as though there is no single best candidate for primary substance. On the one hand, Socrates and Secretariat have the advantage that they actually exist, though their nature is composite. The forms of Socrates and Secretariat, human being and horse, on the other hand, have the advantage that they state the essence of Socrates and Secretariat, *what each of them is*.

Aristotle seems in fact to be asking three different questions. The first is: what *exists*? to which the answer is the individual substance. The second is: what is the *primary cause*, the essence of the individual substance? to which the answer is its form. The third is: what is the principle of explanation in general? to which the answer is the universal. As he puts it later in the *Metaphysics*,

> The primary principles of all things are the actual primary "this" and another thing which exists potentially. The universal causes, then, of which we spoke do not *exist*. For the *individual* is the source of individuals. For while man is the cause of man universally, there *is* no universal man; but

Peleus is the cause of Achilles, and your father of you, and this particular *b* of this particular *ba*, though *b* in general is the cause of *ba* taken without qualification.

(*Metaph.* XII.5, 1071a18–24)

When Aristotle says that the universal causes don't exist, he is countering the Platonic view of Forms as the primary reality. He does not mean that these universal causes are absolutely nothing, however. Universals, for Aristotle, are abstracted from the particulars that exist and function as objects of knowledge. The order of knowledge, which focuses on the universal, is thus somewhat different from the order of being, which is based on the individual. The form of the individual is the link between the two orders.

In his epistemology, just as in his metaphysics, Aristotle tries to bridge the gap between the particular and the universal raised by Plato's "two-worlds" view. Like Plato, Aristotle believes he has an answer to the skeptical problem raised by Socrates. He believes that it is possible for human beings to possess divine wisdom. He moves from sense perception, which is concerned with the attributes of individuals to art and wisdom, which are concerned with the universal form. He presents a number of schemes that explain the connections between perception and reason; one of these occurs in *Metaphysics* Book I, 1–2. According to this passage, the most basic faculty is *sense perception*, which is possessed by all animals. Sense perception is the ability to perceive the sensible attributes of particular objects. Some animals possess *memory* in addition, which makes them able to learn. Human beings in addition to memory possess experience. *Experience* is the ability to apply the lessons learned in memory to a new situation. If one recalls that when Tom and Dick were ill with a cold they took a certain cold medicine with good results, then one can project that Harry will benefit from taking the same drug. So far, we are in the realm of individuals. The next stage of knowledge is *art*; in art one comes to know universals. One learns not only that a certain kind of cold medicine benefits everyone, but also the reason why that is so. Knowing the reason enables the master practitioner in an art (in this case the physician) to teach that art to others. The exact way in which art, the knowledge of the universal, is derived from sensory experience is not easy to understand. It is just a capacity that we have. It is this capacity, though, that makes us rational animals.

The highest art, the most general and abstract and the most difficult to acquire, is *wisdom*. Aristotle defines wisdom in two ways: as understanding of the first principles of reality, and as knowledge of the nature of God, who is the ultimate first principle. God, on Aristotle's view, concerns himself solely with self-knowledge. When we come to know God, we know what God knows, namely God himself; thus, we have divine wisdom. Even wisdom, however, is based ultimately on the perception of individuals. Interestingly, the ultimate object of knowledge, God, is not a universal, but an individual. Like Plato, Aristotle conceives the attainment of wisdom as the result of an ascent from lower experiences through stages to higher ones, until finally one reaches the highest level. Like Plato, he thinks that wisdom is rare and difficult to attain. Both Plato and Aristotle think that the first step in the process begins with sense perception; for Plato, it is sense perception that begins the process of recollection. Unlike Plato, however, who generally denigrates the value of sensory experience, Aristotle does not regard it as inherently deceptive. Both Plato and Aristotle think that sensory experience is basically awareness of particulars, whereas reason is basically awareness of universals. Aristotle mediates the division between sensation and reason with the faculties of memory and experience; Plato, though he does not distinguish these officially, relies on memory in the recollective process. The basic difference between the two, of course, is the one that I have emphasized repeatedly up to this point: for Plato, there are two "worlds," two orders of reality, corresponding to the two mental faculties of knowledge and belief, whereas for Aristotle, there is only one world, a world with sensible as well as intelligible characteristics.

Aristotle's epistemology and metaphysics together constitute an elegant resolution of the problem of separation—of universals and particulars, of reason and sense, of knowledge and belief—created by Plato. This does not mean that there are no problems with his solution. Basically, the Aristotelian synthesis is a compromise between a purely naturalistic view of reality and a view that accepts the existence of non-natural entities, such as Forms. Aristotle wants to extend naturalistic explanation as far as possible, but he also wants to retain the power of the Platonic Forms to explain such things as the nature of knowledge and the meaning of words. When he is criticizing Plato, the naturalistic elements of his thought tend to predominate; but when he talks about reason and knowledge he sounds very much like a Platonist, though admittedly without the Platonic doctrine of separation. Aristotle is a realist about universals, but not an extreme realist, as Plato is. In his epistemology, he tries to combine the best elements of Platonic rationalism, the view that knowledge is a matter of reason, with empiricism, the view that knowledge is derived from experience. Aristotle was thus both a critic of Plato and a dissident Platonist. It is not a surprise that later philosophers emphasized the similarities between the thought of the two philosophers, and treated Aristotle as a Platonist who had an extensive and deep knowledge of nature. Cicero lumps Plato and Aristotle together in *On Moral Ends* as representatives of "the old philosophy."

Aristotelianism survived in the period following Aristotle's death, but his account did not carry the day. The two new schools, Epicureanism and Stoicism, challenged the Aristotelian compromise with more thoroughgoing versions of naturalism. Both schools rejected the realism concerning the existence of universals that Plato and Aristotle had in common. In epistemology, their focus shifts from whether and how we can have knowledge of universals to whether we can have knowledge of particulars. These schools, and Stoicism in particular, propounded theories of knowledge that produced a skeptical response. Aristotle's philosophy underwent a great revival, first at the hands of Islamic philosophers beginning in the eighth century CE, and then by philosophers in Europe in the twelfth and thirteenth centuries, when Aristotle came to have such authority that he was referred to simply as "the philosopher." For the remainder of ancient philosophy, however, Aristotle's voice is merely one among several, and not the most dominant.

## Stoicism, Epicureanism, and Skepticism

The Stoics and Epicureans differ in many respects, but their philosophies have two general similarities: both are *materialists*, and both are *dogmatists*. As *materialists*, they reject the view that Socrates, Plato, and Aristotle all shared: that universals exist outside the mind. They talk instead of "preconceptions" and "concepts," which makes them conceptualists, in terms of the three theories of universals mentioned above; but these mental entities don't "exist" for either school. Universal truths exist, but not universals. What exist, according to the Epicureans, are atoms and the void. The Stoics are even more restrictive: only bodies exist; void is an incorporeal, "not a 'something' but not a 'nothing' either." What I mean by saying that the Epicureans and Stoics are both *dogmatists* is that both schools maintain, with Plato and Aristotle, that there are beliefs (*dogmata*) that we can know with the highest degree of certainty. Socrates, and following him Plato and Aristotle, had made universals the objects of philosophical knowledge. Since the Stoics and Epicureans don't accept the existence of universals, they must ground knowledge, including knowledge of universal truths, in the knowledge of individuals, particulars—that is, in sense perception. Whereas Plato (but not Aristotle) had regarded sense perception as unreliable, the Stoics and Epicureans thought it the very foundation of knowledge, and, therefore, infallible. The Stoics and Epicureans think of knowledge fundamentally differently than do Socrates, Plato, and Aristotle. For Socrates, Plato, and Aristotle, knowledge was something one reached after a long process: though the journey might begin with perception, it did not end there. For the Stoics and Epicureans, on the other hand, certain knowledge was found in perception. Perception was the foundation on which the structure of knowledge was erected.

## Stoicism: Matter

The Stoics held that each body, as well as the body that constitutes the entire universe, the cosmos, is made up of two parts, both of which are physical in nature. There is, first, a passive matter, which is capable of being shaped in an infinite number of ways. Second, there is an active kind of matter, which they identified with fire— not ordinary fire, but what they called a "designing fire"—that works on the passive matter and shapes it into recognizable forms. This Stoic distinction is similar to Aristotle's distinction between form and matter, except that both components are material. Why is this so? Because the Stoics thought that only a body could act on a body. If the "form" or organizing principle of a body acted on it, that form must be another body. The Stoics raise here a major objection both to Platonic and Aristotelian metaphysics. Aristotle had objected to Plato's Forms that they could not be causes because they were not *in* the things that participated in them. The Stoics raise a similar objection to Aristotle: even if the forms are in things, if they are not material components of those things, how can they be causes? This active form of matter, this designing fire, corresponds to Aristotle's moving, formal, and final causes. Its designing work is *teleological* in nature: it organizes the passive matter with an end in view. Purpose is "built in" to the structure of each thing, and this is as true of the universe as a whole as it is of the particular things in it. In the universe of the Stoics, nothing happens by chance. Everything is ordered for the good of the whole.

## Epicureanism: matter

The materialism of the Epicureans is more radical in this respect than that of the Stoics. The Epicureans reject the idea of teleology altogether. The Epicureans were atomists.

### ATOMISM

Atomism is the view that nothing ultimately exists except atoms and void. It arose in response to the challenge of Parmenides. Parmenides had argued that, as *not-being* is impossible (not-being=nothing, and nothing does not exist), all that is real must be a single motionless being, like a sphere. The atomists cut the Gordian knot of Parmenides' argument by boldly positing that not-being exists just as much as being. By "not-being," the atomists meant space, which they conceived of as infinite and in itself completely devoid of being. Being, in contrast, they thought of as extremely small, invisible particles, completely devoid of not-being, infinite in number, perpetually moving about in infinite space. These particles they called "atoms"— the Greek word *atomos* means "uncuttable." Ancient atomism is the ancestor of modern atomic theory, which originated with John Dalton in 1805. The picture of the atom as a solid, indivisible particle persisted until early in the twentieth century, when it was discovered that atoms were made of more elementary particles.

About the first atomist, Leucippus, very little is known. Much better known is his student Democritus of Abdera, who lived from about 460 to about 370. Atomism, as developed by these two thinkers, is a materialist philosophy: nothing exists except matter, in the form of atoms, and the medium (empty space) in which it moves. The atomists thought the atoms and space to be uncreated and indestructible, but they thought that clusters of atoms, formed by chance collisions, created particular world-orders, which come into being and pass away. Chance and necessity, not divine providence, are the principles that govern the universe. Though there are gods, they do not interfere with its operation. Souls are material parts of living organisms.

Epicurus followed Democritus in most respects, but he made one important innovation. Democritus had thought that atoms moved naturally in all directions; Epicurus said that they naturally moved in one direction: "downward" through infinite space. (What sense it makes to talk of "up" and "down" in infinite space is not clear.) At random intervals, an atom may "swerve" slightly and become entangled with another. From these entanglements, the various world-orders are formed. All of the complexity of our cosmos, and of the infinite number of other world-orders he thought existed, resulted from the random combinations of atoms. Because the swerve was random, it introduced indeterminism into what otherwise would have been a universe completely determined by the movement of atoms. If ancient atomism in general was the ancestor of modern atomic theory, the doctrine of the swerve seems to resemble to some degree the random decay of the trans-uranic elements. The doctrine of the swerve had ethical implications for Epicurus: he saw it as making free will possible. In general, the atomic theory had therapeutic implications: by removing anxiety about the causal intervention of the gods, it made tranquility possible.

## Stoicism: knowledge

The Stoic and Epicurean theories of matter have implications for their views of the soul, free will, and the nature of the cosmos, which I'll discuss in subsequent chapters. I want to turn now to the second area of generic agreement between the schools: their accounts of knowledge. As I noted above, the Stoics divided philosophy into three branches: ethics, physics, and logic. Their account of knowledge was part of logic. (The Stoics made important contributions to what we call "logic": the theory of the formal analysis of rational arguments.) You will recall that the centerpiece of Stoic ethics was the concept of the sage. The sage is supposed never to be mistaken, to be infallible. Let's consider this alleged infallibility in general, and then discuss how it is supposed to apply in ethics. The most basic element of Stoic epistemology is the appearance or impression. Now an impression is a mental event, but an event of a particular kind. An impression *represents* something as being the case in reality. An impression appears to be "imprinted" on the soul by something in the world. Impressions have what we would call *intentionality*, "aboutness." They appear to be *about* something other than themselves. Some impressions are such that we might have doubts about them. For instance, we might say of something partially hidden from us in nearby bushes, "That appears to be a cat, but—I don't know—it could be a squirrel." On the other hand, some impressions, say the Stoics, are such that we *cannot* be mistaken about them. Suppose now that it's *my* cat that we're talking about, and he's sitting on my lap in broad daylight. Can I be mistaken about that? The Stoics thought not. They called such impressions "gripping." A gripping impression is not one that we grip; it is one that grips us. A gripping impression is caused by something real, it represents that thing exactly as it is, and it could not be caused by something other than what it purports to represent. Nothing could cause my impression of my cat, sitting on my lap in broad daylight, except my cat. If I am presented with the statement "My cat is sitting on my lap," I will endorse that statement: I will, in Stoic terms, *assent* to it.

The Stoics used the gripping impression to distinguish the judgments of the sane from the insane: the insane had impressions that may have felt gripping to them, but which were not in fact gripping, for they were not representations of reality and they were not rational. This makes it sound as if the sane person is the standard of judgment, but things are not that simple. It is at this point that the sage enters the picture, and, although we might imagine that sane people abound, the sage is a rarity, if one exists at all. The infallibility of the sage consists in the fact that he *only* assents to impressions that are gripping. Most of us may assent to gripping impressions some of the time, but we will sometimes assent where we shouldn't, and prove to be mistaken. Not the sage. If knowledge is based on truth, and if the gripping impression is the criterion of truth, the judgments of the sage are those that are based on truth, not opinion. The sage, said the Stoics, does not opine; he does not give assent to non-gripping impressions. The Stoics concluded that the idea that sanity is widespread while sages are rare is mistaken: only the sage is sane. Everyone else is mad. (The Stoics were fond of these paradoxical judgments: only the sage is free, only the sage is king, and so forth.)

At this point, we can see the ethical dimensions of the gripping impression. One kind of impression that all of us have at one time or another is the impression that some state of affairs, most likely something happening to ourselves or someone near and dear to us, is good or bad. We win the lottery, and we think that is good; we are diagnosed with cancer, and we think that is bad. These impressions may appear to us to be gripping; caught up in our emotions of elation or gloom, we believe that they tell us something about reality. The sage knows, on the other hand, that such impressions are *indifferent*: a preferred indifferent, in the case of wealth, a dispreferred indifferent in the case of disease. The sage will not find these impressions gripping, and will not, accordingly, assent to them. The sage will align his will perfectly with the cosmic order. Since the cosmic order is, for the Stoics, the expression of the divine will, the sage will possess divine wisdom.

## Epicureanism: knowledge

Epicurus, as in his theory of matter, was here again more radical than the Stoics. The branch of Epicurean philosophy that dealt with questions of knowledge was called "canonic," from the Greek word *kanôn*, literally meaning "measuring rod" and by extension "measure" or "standard." Here Epicurus departed from Democritus. Democritus had held that our perceptions, and in particular our perceptions of sensible properties of things, did not correspond to the real nature of things. As he put it, "*by convention* sweet, *by convention* bitter, *by convention* hot, *by convention* cold, *by convention* color: but *in reality* atoms and void" (fr. 9; my italics). Democritus was a *reductionist* concerning these sensible properties, and we may assume that he was a reductionist about the other things that we discern with our senses, such as oranges and automobiles. Such things might *appear* to us to exist, but what *really* exist are atoms and the void. According to Democritean atomism, sensory qualities do not directly reveal the true nature of the world. This created a tension in Democritus' version of atomism between the senses and reason. Reason tells us that only atoms and the void exist; the senses tell us that sensible things and their properties exist. But the senses provide the only evidence we have in favor of atomism. Democritus had pictured the senses objecting to reason: "Wretched mind, do you take your assurances from us and then overthrow us? Our overthrow is your downfall" (fr. 125).

Epicurus took a different tack. He made the senses the *canon*, the criterion or standard of truth. According to Epicurus, *all* sense impressions are true. Each of the five senses, operating in its own sphere, was held to be infallible. Now this infallibility applies only to the immediate objects of sensation: the shape, texture, taste, smell, and appearance of an orange, for instance; in general, the "look and feel" of it. The existence of the real orange is something we infer from these sensible properties. Still, that means that sensible properties have to exist, not merely appear to exist. Yet these properties, which we perceive, cannot be the same things as atoms, which we do not perceive. How can we explain their existence? Here Epicurus offered a physical account of the process of perception. Focusing primarily on visual perception, but including at least hearing and smell also, Epicurus claimed that objects were constantly emitting very fine films of particles that retain the shape or character of the object. These films strike the sense organ (e.g. the eye) of the person, causing him or her to perceive the object. Even though these films are made up of atoms, which we don't see, these atoms are arranged in complex structures. The sensible properties that we do see are caused by these complex structures. They *emerge* from those complex structures; thus, the Epicureans are referred to as "emergentists." Emergentism is contrasted with Democritean reductionism: whereas for Democritus only atoms and the void are real, for emergentists such as Epicurus not only atoms and the void, but also the complex structures they produce and the sensible properties that these in turn produce are real. Normally, this causal process is error-free; however, when an object is viewed from a distance, the films may be altered by the medium through which they pass, causing, in the most frequently cited example, a square tower seen from a distance to appear round. In this way, Epicurus resolved the tension between the senses and reason that had troubled Democritus.

One difficulty with this account of infallibility is that it applies only to sensible properties. How can we infer from this the existence and nature of the actual orange? How can I know that there is a real orange "out there," independent of my experience of it? The Epicurean answer is that we can't, at least not infallibly. Rather, the mind forms a judgment about the existence and nature of the orange, based on the sensory images it receives. It compares these data of our senses with ideas of the orange it has already stored in memory from previous experiences; the Epicureans called these ideas "preconceptions." They thought that these preconceptions were also true; they were derived from sensations in a process that sounds like the discovery of the universal in Aristotle. As in Aristotle, they provide meaning for terms such as "orange." In the process of evaluating our sensations in light of our preconceptions, however, errors can occur. I may know perfectly well what an orange is, but apply this preconception incorrectly, perhaps to a sensation produced by a tangerine. Thus, judgment or opinion is fallible, though sensation is infallible.

This physical account of perception that Epicurus gives offers an explanation of perception and perceptual error, though one that is subject to questions, both skeptical and physical. On the physical side, one may wonder how the surface of physical objects, some of which can be quite large, can produce images small enough to affect the sense organ of the perceiver. Moreover, the apparent size of the object must vary with the distance, so that the Parthenon seen from a long way off must appear small, while when it is perceived from up close it must appear large; yet the film in each case must be equally small, small enough to impact the sense organ. The second problem is more fundamental. Do our sense impressions, derived from these films, correspond to reality at all? If all we experience are these films, how do we know *what* causes them? Even if these films have an external cause, how can we know that they *resemble* that cause? This is a problem that can be generalized: it is just as much a problem for the Stoics as for the Epicureans. Both schools adhere to a *causal* or a *representative* conception of knowledge. They hold that the sense impressions of which I am directly aware are caused by things in the world of which I am not directly aware. Looking out at the world "from the inside," with direct access only to my impressions and conceptions or preconceptions, how can I know that these impressions correspond to, are caused by, things in the real world that resemble them? To put matters in terms of the sharp dichotomy posed by the Stoics, how do I know that I am not mad, or perhaps dreaming? (The French philosopher René Descartes raised exactly these objections at the start of the modern era of philosophy, setting off centuries of philosophical debate.)

## Skepticism

It is just here, between the image and the reality that causes it, that skepticism can drive its wedge.

## SKEPTICISM

Skepticism is a philosophical view that doubts or denies claims to knowledge. While Xenophanes of Colophon, a Presocratic philosopher who lived from about 570 to about 475 BCE, and Socrates expressed sentiments that are skeptical in nature, the birth of skepticism as a distinct philosophy is credited to Pyrrho of Elis, who lived from about 360 to about 270. Pyrrho wrote nothing. His disciple Timon of Phlius wrote down his teachings, but only fragments of his writings survive. Pyrrho seems to have said that we can have no knowledge of reality, and must confine ourselves to appearances. He may have advocated a life without belief (a very controversial doctrine whose exact meaning is still debated today). He seems also to have thought that such a life would lead to peace of mind, which he held to be the goal or end of philosophical investigation. This idea that philosophy is therapeutic in its goal becomes a central characteristic of Hellenistic philosophy.

Two schools of skeptical thought emerge in the centuries following Pyrrho. The first is the Academic school, which arose in Plato's Academy in the third century in response to the dogmatic philosophy of the Stoics. Academic skepticism traced its origin to Socrates, who denied that he had any knowledge or wisdom. The Academics (who did not refer to themselves as skeptics)—first Arcesilaus (who lived from about 316 to about 241 and was head of the Academy in the middle years of the third century), and then Carneades (214–129/8), head of the Academy for the last thirty years or so of his life—argued against the Stoic view that certain, infallible knowledge is possible. Like some other ancient philosophers, including Socrates (who was the inspiration for Academic skepticism) and Pyrrho, these two philosophers wrote nothing; their views have to be extracted from the works of later writers, such as Cicero. Carneades is thought to have gone beyond mere denial of the Stoic theory of knowledge to develop a constructive theory of knowledge based on claims that were convincing, worthy of acceptance, though uncertain.

Pyrrhonian skepticism acknowledges Pyrrho rather than Socrates as its founder, but it shares many features with Academic skepticism. Aenesidemus (first century BCE) and Agrippa (first or second century CE) devised whole batteries of arguments, referred to as modes, designed to attack belief. As with other figures above, we know the work of these philosophers because they have been preserved by a later writer, in this case Sextus Empiricus (about

160 to 210). Sextus wrote two works: the *Outlines of Pyrrhonism* and *Against the Mathematicians;* it is through these two works that ancient Pyrrhonism came to be known in the West during the Renaissance. Academic and Pyrrhonian skepticism were hugely influential in the modern era of philosophy (roughly 1640–1800). They remain controversial even today.

The Academic skeptics attacked the fundamental notion of Stoic epistemology, the gripping impression. There is no impression, they claimed, however "gripping" it may appear, that could not have been caused by something other than what appears to have caused it. Granted, it looks like my cat is seated on my lap, but how can I be certain I am not mad, or dreaming? If there are no gripping impressions, then we are never justified in assenting to an impression, and, if there is no such thing as justified assent, then there can be no Stoic sage. Absolute certainty is impossible; up to this point they agreed with Pyrrho. One Academic, in particular, however, put forward a view that attempted to mitigate the extreme skepticism of Pyrrho. That was Carneades. He argued that, although there was no gripping impression, no absolutely certain foundation of knowledge, we can have, if we give up the ideal of certainty, a kind of knowledge that is less than certain. We can have, if not absolute truth, then a reasonable approximation to it.

While rejecting the idea of a gripping impression, Carneades claimed that some impressions were *convincing* or *plausible*. It was the convincing impression, Carneades argued, that was the criterion of truth. Convincing impressions might prove to be incorrect or misleading, but they warrant our tentative acceptance. Convincing impressions could be subject to further testing, however; they could be *corroborated* or *uncontroverted*. The more corroboration an impression received, the stronger the belief formed on its basis would be. Finally, an impression and its corresponding belief might be "thoroughly investigated," examined and tested from all sides. Such a thoroughly investigated belief would have the best claim to be knowledge of any belief that it was possible for a human being to attain. It would not be divine wisdom, but human; but it would be more than Socrates' admission of his ignorance. Carneades was so cagy about his actual beliefs that even his closest disciples could not be sure what they were. This account of knowledge, however, is associated with his name, whether it reflected his actual view or not. This view of knowledge is probabilistic, or perhaps "plausibilistic," fallibilistic, holistic, and coherentist. That is, our best, most considered judgments, judgments we would say we know to be true, are only the most plausible or probable given the evidence, though they still might prove to be false. They are to be judged as part of our whole body of beliefs, and on the basis of their internal coherence with our other beliefs. Truth is still understood as correspondence between an impression or belief and an external reality, but the practical test for the truth of our beliefs is their coherence with the system of our beliefs, taken as a whole.

To illustrate the distinction between the Stoic and the Academic criteria of truth, we might make use of the concept of the "master detective" from fiction. The Stoic detective, in investigating a crime, might fasten upon a single piece of evidence that, he says, points inevitably, with certainty, to the guilt of a particular person. The Academic detective, on the other hand, would regard all the alleged evidence as problematic; some of it might be convincing and very difficult to reject, but the detective will only accept the evidence if it fits into a pattern with all the other available pieces of evidence. Even then, the detective must conduct an investigation to ensure that matters have been "thoroughly investigated," and that no stone has been left unturned. Only then will the Academic detective reach a conclusion about the guilt or innocence of a particular suspect; and even then, though the certainty of the detective might be sufficient to procure the arrest and conviction of the suspect, the Academic detective will regard his identification of the suspect as falling short of absolute certainty. The difficulty in deciding between these two models of knowledge is that detective fiction, and probably reality, abounds with examples of each kind of detective. Sometimes the two models are embodied in a single person. The Academic detective seems more judicious than the Stoic, relying on the coherence of impressions and their thorough investigation, in contrast to the dogmatism of the Stoic; but can't the Stoic detective rely on the investigative techniques of the Academic detective, while still holding that some evidence rises to the status of a gripping impression?

The ancient battle between skeptical and dogmatist schools did not end in a clear victory for either side. Eventually, in the late ancient world (the third through fifth centuries), Platonism became the dominant philosophy, and the skeptical debate went onto the back burner for over a millennium (though St. Augustine, a Christian Platonist, wrote a little book entitled *Against the Academics* in about 386 CE). The skeptical problems raised by Pyrrho and Sextus, Arcesilaus and Carneades had to wait until the Renaissance to be revived. From the time of Montaigne down to the middle years of the twentieth century, the attempt to refute the skeptic took center stage, dominating discussions in epistemology. Though it has ceased to be, in recent years, the one absolutely central topic in epistemology, it continues to be seriously discussed today. The legacy of Pyrrho and Sextus, Arcesilaus and Carneades, and their dogmatic opponents has proved to be surprisingly durable; the skeptical debate is one of the lasting legacies of ancient philosophy.

# 3
# The soul

*What has happened to me may well be a good thing, and those of us who believe death to be an evil are certainly mistaken. ... There is good hope that death ... is one of two things: either the dead are nothing and have no perception of anything, or it is, as we are told, a change and a relocating for the soul from here to another place.*

(Plato's *Apology*)

## Socrates

Philosophy, as Socrates understood it, was care of the soul, something different from the pursuit of wealth, reputation, and honors—and, I would add, pleasure and power. Care of the soul involves thinking about wisdom and truth. But why should we concern ourselves with the condition of our soul? Why not pursue pleasure and power instead of wisdom? Socrates offers two basic reasons why we should put care of our soul above those, and indeed all other goals. The first reason is intrinsic to the nature of the soul; the second concerns the consequences that may befall the soul after death if we neglect to care for it in life. He discusses the first reason in a brief passage in the *Crito*, usually considered a companion piece to the *Apology* (it is set in prison where Socrates is awaiting execution following his trial). Socrates compares care of the body to care of the soul. If we don't eat, drink, or exercise properly, says Socrates, we will ruin our body. If, on the other hand, we don't act properly with regard to the just and unjust, shameful and beautiful, or good and evil—in other words, if we don't act ethically—we will ruin our soul, which is much more valuable than the body. In either case, life will not be worth living. Just existing isn't sufficient to make a life worthwhile, according to Socrates; only a life in which one's body and soul are in good condition is so. Unjust, shameful, and evil acts directly, intrinsically damage our soul, the most precious part of us. For that reason, we ought to devote our energy to acquiring wisdom about care of the soul. This, of course, requires the method of search described in chapter 1.

The second reason to care for one's soul is stated at the end of the *Apology*. As the quotation above indicates, Socrates asserted that death must be either a perpetual loss of consciousness, a state in which the dead are "nothing," or transfer of the soul to a different location. That location is Hades, and Socrates offers a brief account of life there. First, he says he expects to be judged by true judges, unlike the judges who voted for his conviction. Second, he hopes to continue his examination of people there, with the aim of finding out whether anyone is wise. The lives of the inhabitants of Hades are better than our lives here (they are *eudaimonesteron*, more *eudaimôn*, he says; this is a passage where "happier" is probably the best translation); and they are deathless as well, "if indeed what we are told is true." Socrates' portrait of life in Hades recalls Homer's in Book 11 of the *Odyssey*, composed three hundred years earlier. In the *Odyssey*, Odysseus is sent by the sorceress Circe to Hades to consult with the prophet Teiresias about how to return to his home in Ithaca. In the course of this journey, Odysseus encounters several of the people that Socrates also mentions as inhabiting the underworld:

Agamemnon, Ajax, and Sisyphus. Homer mentions Minos acting as a judge among the dead, and he is one of four judges Socrates mentions by name—the others are Rhadamanthus, Aeacus, and Triptolemus. In both Socrates' account and Homer's, the dead retain the identities they possessed in life, and the source of that identity is the continued existence of one and the same soul. This soul is immortal: Homer places no term on its existence.

But Socrates' account of life in Hades differs from Homer's in four significant ways. First, the dead are happier than those on earth, according to Socrates. Homer's dead, in contrast, are miserable. When Odysseus encounters Teiresias in the underworld, the first question he hears from him is why he has left earth to come to Hades, "this place without pleasure" (*Od.* 11, 94). When he meets Achilles, the greatest of the Greek heroes of the Trojan War, Achilles tells Odysseus, "I would rather follow the plow as thrall to another man, one with no land allotted to him and not much to live on, than be a king over all the perished dead" (*Od.* 11, 489–91). This miserable state of the dead is probably due to a second difference, the fact that all of them (except Teiresias, says Circe) have lost their wits, their intelligence. They are, as Circe says, "flittering shadows." Achilles asks Odysseus, "How could you endure to come down here to Hades' place, where the senseless dead men dwell, mere imitations of perished mortals?" (*Od.* 11, 474–6). Only when they have drunk blood is their intelligence restored and they can speak to Odysseus. Socrates, however, expects to carry on conversations with the souls of the dead. A third difference concerns the judgment of the dead. Homer shows Minos issuing judgments *among* the dead, but he does not describe a general judgment *of* the dead, such as Socrates describes. Homer shows three figures—Tityus, Tantalus, and Sisyphus—undergoing perpetual punishment in Hades, but most of the inhabitants are not there as punishment; they are in Hades simply because it is where the soul goes when it dies. Fourth, according to Homer, the soul is a kind of breath, *pneuma*, that is responsible for the life of the individual human being. When humans die, their souls leave their bodies—they "expire," breathe their last breath—and travel to the underworld, Hades, where they continue to exist, but in a shadowy, insubstantial form. When Odysseus meets his mother in Hades, she explains to him the nature of death: when people die, "the soul flitters out" from the body "like a dream and flies away." Socrates does not tell us anything about the material composition of the soul. He only tells us what the soul does and why care of the soul is important.

Homer doesn't argue for his view of the soul. He's a poet, after all, not a philosopher. Perhaps he is just giving expression to common Greek beliefs. Homer doesn't explain why, if the soul is a kind of breath, and if it travels without damage to Hades, it doesn't preserve its intellect, its reasoning power. He doesn't explain how something like breath can be alive in the first place, or can reason. Nor does he explain what it means for the souls in Hades to retain their earthly identities. Nonetheless, there is no doubt that both philosophers and ordinary people were influenced by the Homeric view of the soul, especially the claims that the soul is immortal and that it remains, in the afterlife, the same person it had been in life. We see this influence in Socrates' account of the afterlife in the *Apology*. I think it is safe to say that the predominant view of the soul among non-philosophers in the classical age, even in the heyday of ancient philosophy, was more or less Homer's. People live, they die, their souls go to Hades, where they continue to exist, but in a kind of living death.

Socrates' account of the afterlife of the soul is, he says in the *Apology*, one of two possibilities, the other being extinction, or permanent loss of consciousness. In other dialogues, this alternative is quietly shelved: we hear no more of it. It is the idea of continued existence in Hades that Socrates endorses. He affirms the soul's immortality and its continued existence in the underworld in the *Crito* and the *Gorgias*. At the beginning of the *Crito*, Socrates recounts a dream in which a white-robed woman predicts his imminent arrival in the underworld. At the end of the dialogue, he imagines the laws of Athens speaking to him, saying that he should value goodness above all other things, even above the welfare of his own children, so that when he arrives in Hades he can use that as his defense. At the end of the *Gorgias*, Socrates caps a long argument over the best life for a human being with an imaginative account of the afterlife that expands on the *Apology* model without really altering it. First of all, he assigns the task of judging the dead to three of the four judges that he had mentioned in the *Apology*: Minos, Rhadamanthus, and Aeacus. Second, in the *Gorgias*, Socrates explains the result of the judgment of the dead: the righteous go to the Isles of the Blessed, while the wicked go to Tartarus for punishment.

What is the status of this story? In the *Phaedo*, *Republic*, and *Phaedrus*, Plato frequently uses myths to describe the afterlife, and this looks like one such myth. That does not necessarily mean that Plato thinks it is imaginative fiction, a kind of fairy tale. To call something a myth in the ancient world is not necessarily to suggest that it is false; it is rather to indicate that it is an imaginative narrative, a story, rather than a rational argument. Plato's myths are intended to contain a core of truth, though finding that truth may require some interpretive digging. Yet Socrates says explicitly at the start of the story that he considers it a *logos*, a rational account, rather than a *mythos*, a myth; he claims further that the story is *true*. At the end of the account, he says that he is *convinced* by it. These claims fall short of *knowledge claims*: Socrates does not claim *infallible certainty* about the story, but they come close. They are not mere conjecture or hypothesis in his opinion. Perhaps he is not committed to the various details of the story, but this remark seems to imply that he believes that its main points—the immortality of the soul, the judgment of the soul after death by fair judges, and the system of rewards and punishments—are correct.

The *Gorgias* contains an important definition of death: death is "nothing but the separation of two things from each other, the soul and the body" (*Grg.* 524b). This definition suggests, if it does not actually imply, that soul and body are different *sorts* of thing: the body being material in nature and the soul not. This would be one of the places where Socrates departs from Homer, who thought of the soul as a kind of matter, namely breath. This definition is the basis of an account of the nature of the soul that *Plato* develops in later dialogues. This account is known as psychophysical *dualism*, the view that body and soul are two different kinds of thing, two separate substances. Dualism is ideally suited to explain the immortality of the soul: these substances, says Plato, are capable of existing apart from each other. The variety of dualism Socrates and Plato defend is *interactionism*: the claim that these two separate substances act on each other. The body generates sensations, which inform the soul of certain facts, and the soul acts on the body accordingly. For example, my body generates the sensation of hunger; my soul directs my body to go looking for food. In general, it is the soul that is in charge of the body; though the body plays an important role in the life of a person, it is the soul that is, or ought to be, the body's ruler.

Where the ancient philosophers spoke of the relation between body and soul, modern philosophers prefer to speak of the relation between body and *mind*. It has been said that most non-philosophers even today think of the relation of the mind and body as dualistic in nature. Dualism may be built into the very concept of the mind. There is a major conceptual difficulty with dualism, however, that has made it unacceptable to many philosophers, including some in the ancient world, as we shall see later in this chapter. It is that dualism cannot explain how interaction between two substances of such different kinds can occur. How can anything but a body act on another body? philosophers have objected. If the soul is a kind of breath, as Homer said, then interaction is possible, but how is it possible if the soul is immaterial? Despite Homer's view, the non-material nature of the soul seems necessary for immortality, so that, if the soul is material, it would seem to be impossible for it to be immortal. It seems that we are faced with a choice: a material, mortal soul that can interact with the body or an immaterial, immortal soul that can't. For the dualist, the interaction of the soul with the body is something that can't be understood. It is a mystery.

# Plato

As I have said previously, it is difficult to know where Socrates ends and Plato begins. It is particularly difficult in the case of the soul. Plato's views develop out of Socrates', and, though there are significant differences between Socrates' view and the view that Plato ultimately develops, I think Socrates would see the kernel of his view of the soul in those developments. If we consider the *Apology*, *Crito*, and *Gorgias* to represent Socrates' view of the soul, then Socrates' legacy to Plato consists of four main claims: that the soul is immortal, that it retains its personal identity after death, that it is judged after death and rewarded or punished based on its conduct in life, and that death is the separation of the soul and the body. The latter claim at the very least suggests the dualist conception of the soul. The judgment of the soul seems to require a concept of moral responsibility, and this in turn seems to require the idea that the soul is the bearer of personal identity, for it is not fair to judge someone for past actions unless that very person was responsible for those actions. The soul is the center of agency for Socrates: when the person acts, it is the soul of the person acting through the means of the body.

Socrates is certainly the major influence on Plato's conception of the soul. There is a second influence, however, that is almost as important. That is Pythagoreanism. Pythagoras was an early Presocratic philosopher, born around 570. He established a school of followers, who out of loyalty attributed their own philosophical and mathematical discoveries (such as the famous

"Pythagorean theorem") to the master. Though it is difficult to say where Pythagoras' own contributions end and where those of his disciples begin, one thing scholars are confident in attributing to Pythagoras is his view of the soul: the soul is immortal and reincarnated; it transmigrates into another body, perhaps the body of an animal, after death. Pythagoras does not say explicitly that the soul is immaterial, but his doctrine of the transfer of the soul from one body to another depends on a contrast between body and soul that certainly suggests that it is. Pythagoras thought that the soul existed apart from the body, for it left one body and entered another. Pythagoras may have been the first psycho-physical dualist in the Western philosophical tradition. He certainly seems to be a direct ancestor of Plato in this respect.

Once Plato becomes familiar with the Pythagorean doctrine of the soul, he integrates it with the conception he inherited from Socrates. How did that occur? Plato made three voyages to Sicily, in 388, 367, and 361, in the vain hope of converting the ruler of Syracuse, initially Dionysius I and later his son Dionysius II, to philosophy. In the course of the first of these trips, he made the acquaintance of members of the Pythagorean brotherhood. It is after this date, interpreters believe, that Pythagorean influences begin to exist side-by-side with Socratic in Plato's dialogues. Some interpreters see Pythagorean influence in the account of immortality at the end of the *Gorgias*; it is certainly present in two subsequent dialogues, the *Meno* and the *Phaedo*. Beginning with the *Meno*, and continuing through the late *Timaeus*, Pythagoreanism plays a major role in Plato's philosophy. In the *Meno*, you will recall, Socrates and Meno have been inquiring into the nature of virtue. When all of Meno's attempts at defining virtue fail, he expresses his frustration by asking Socrates how it is possible to inquire into any subject: if one already knows the answer, there is no need to inquire, but, if one does not know the answer, how will one know it even if one comes right up against it? Socrates replies with his doctrine of recollection, discussed in chapter 2. He claims to have heard from certain "wise men and women ... priests and priestesses whose care it is to be able to give an account of their practices" that "the human soul is immortal; at times it comes to an end, which they call dying, at times it is reborn, but it is never destroyed" (*Meno* 81a–b). It seems plausible that the "priests and priestesses" to whom he attributes the doctrine are members of the Pythagorean brotherhood. The part of the doctrine of recollection that concerns the immortality and reincarnation of the soul certainly looks like it comes straight from Pythagoreanism. Once introduced, however, reincarnation becomes Platonic doctrine, repeated first in the *Phaedo*, then at the end of the *Republic*, then in the *Phaedrus*, *Timaeus*, and *Laws*.

What Plato does, I think, is to take these two conceptions of the soul, the Socratic and the Pythagorean, integrate them, and add some new developments of his own. I shall refer below to the "Socratic-Pythagorean" conception of the soul. I do not mean to suggest by this that Socrates was influenced in his view of the soul by Pythagoras, only that the two conceptions of the soul were combined in the mind of Plato, specifically in the *Meno*. These new developments increase the complexity of his view of the soul, and cause some modifications in the Socratic–Pythagorean portrait, but he retains much of that portrait down to his latest works. Plato's modifications of the Socratic-Pythagorean conception of the soul occur in several areas. First, Plato offers us a bevy of arguments in favor of the immortality of the soul. Second, and related to the first, he integrates Socratic-Pythagorean psychology with his own metaphysics. Third, he makes the nature of the soul more complex. Fourth, he modifies the Socratic-Pythagorean view of personal identity. Finally, he offers a conception of the soul as self-mover that is only implicit in his earlier accounts of the soul. Let's examine each of these developments in turn.

First, Plato offers several arguments for the immortality of the soul. Before the *Phaedo*, neither Socrates nor Pythagoras nor

Plato had presented any *arguments* for the immortality of the soul. Socrates had presented an argument in the *Apology* that death was a good thing, and one part of the argument had stated the possibility that the soul continued its existence in Hades, but he had not argued for the truth of that possibility. In the *Gorgias*, he said that his story of the afterlife was a rational account, but the account itself was a description, not an argument. In the *Meno*, when the doctrine of recollection is added to the Socratic portrait of the soul, the immortality of the soul is asserted but not defended by argument. All of that changes in the *Phaedo*. The *Phaedo* is Plato's most thorough discussion of the nature of the soul, though it does not give us his last word on the topic. It is the one Platonic dialogue explicitly devoted to the question of the immortality of the soul. The central core of the dialogue is a series of arguments in favor of immortality. Plato may be implicitly acknowledging the influence of Pythagoreanism on his thought by casting as Socrates' two chief interlocutors in the *Phaedo* Simmias and Cebes, visitors from Thebes and associates of the Pythagorean philosopher Philolaus. Whereas in the *Meno* the immortality of the soul was something assumed as part of the doctrine of recollection, in the *Phaedo* we find the phenomenon of recollection used to prove the immortality of the soul, or at least its existence before birth.

The discussion of the soul in the *Phaedo* emerges from the context of the dialogue: the day of Socrates' execution. Socrates is in prison, surrounded by his friends (excluding Plato, who was absent due to illness). Socrates attempts to show them that they should not think of his death as a source of sorrow, but rather as something about which they should be cheerful. Philosophy, says Socrates, is the practice of dying (or training for death). Death, as was noted in the *Gorgias*, is the separation of the soul from the body. What happens to each substance after death? The body is just a corpse, which eventually decays. The soul, on the other hand, remains in the condition it was in when embodied. It has to undergo purification so as to be cleansed of its past wrong-doing. The same process of purification had been described in the *Gorgias* but it was not clear there what the purpose of purification was. This question is answered in the *Phaedo*: the soul must be purified so that it may be reincarnated. The philosopher is not concerned with goods of the body, but with goods of the soul. The philosopher's concern is with knowledge, and the senses are only impediments to knowledge. The philosopher seeks understanding of the Forms—Socrates mentions "the Just itself ... and the Beautiful and the Good," as well as "the reality of all other things, that which each of them essentially is" (*Phd.* 65d). These objects are not properly pursued by means of sense perception, but by "pure thought," which "track[s] down each reality pure and by itself"; pure thought requires the separation of the soul from the body. The separation of the soul from the body occurs in death; therefore, the soul desires death.

Socrates makes several arguments for the immortality of the soul in the *Phaedo*. Four of them involve the theory of Forms. In addition to the passage just mentioned, there is the argument, mentioned above, involving recollection; the passage almost immediately following it, where he says that the soul is likely to be immortal because it resembles the unchanging Forms rather than the changing world of sensible things; and the final argument, where Socrates presents a general theory of explanation. As a young man, he says, he had been very interested in the philosophy of nature. He had wondered about such issues as what causes the decay of living creatures, what causes thought, what causes growth; he relates these questions to others that seem to us to be quite different, not physical but logical or conceptual: what makes one man seem taller than another "by a head," and what makes ten greater than eight. He became confused about the answers that some of his predecessors had given to these questions. Then he heard one day someone reading from a book by Anaxagoras, who had stated that Mind was the cause of all things. He was excited by this prospect because he assumed that Mind would order all things for the best, with an end in view: that is, teleologically, for some purpose. He found, however, that Anaxagoras made no use of the teleological principle, but gave mechanical, physiological explanations for change. Socrates says that it was as if, in trying to explain why he was in prison, one had explained how his bones and sinews enabled him to sit and move, but had ignored the real cause or reason, namely that the Athenians had thought it better to convict him and he had thought it better to submit to their punishment than to escape.

Socrates says that he would be happy to have an explanation of the kind that Anaxagoras had promised but not delivered. (Plato would later provide such an explanation in the *Timaeus*.) Instead, he developed a "second-best" explanation, the theory of Forms. First, he posited the existence of a Beautiful, a Good, a Large, and "all the rest." Then he proposed that, "if there is anything beautiful besides the Beautiful itself, it is for no other reason than that it shares in that Beautiful, and ... so with everything" (*Phd.* 100c). He rejects all other explanations but clings, "simply, naively and foolishly," to the explanation that *nothing else* makes something beautiful, good or in general *F*, but the participation of that thing in Beauty, Goodness, or, again in general, *F*-ness. When change occurs, that change is understood simply as something's coming to participate, or ceasing to participate, in a Form.

This is the initial version of Socrates' theory of explanation, but from it he develops a more sophisticated version. Socrates presents this version in terms of Forms that are opposites. Odd and Even are opposites. Three and Two are not opposites, but Two is essentially even and Three is essentially odd. When something comes to participate in Two, it also comes to participate in Even. Likewise, snow is by its nature cold, and fire is by its nature hot. When something catches fire, it becomes hot. When snow falls, it is cold. What is the application of this sophisticated version of the theory of causation to soul? Life and death are opposites. Soul is

not identical to life, but soul is essentially connected to the Form
of Life. Therefore, whenever soul enters a body, it brings life with
it. When it leaves a body, it takes life with it. The presence of soul
is incompatible with the presence of death. The soul, therefore,
is essentially deathless, essentially alive. What is deathless is indestructible; therefore, the soul, being by its very nature deathless
and indestructible, must be immortal. Following this final argument for the immortality of the soul, the *Phaedo* concludes with
an elaborate myth, similar to the account at the end of the *Gorgias*,
of the fate of the soul after death. It includes a detailed geography
of the earth, including the underworld. Once he begins to argue
for immortality, he continues the practice in later dialogues: there
are arguments for immortality in *Republic* X and in the *Phaedrus*.
We shall examine the *Phaedrus* argument below.

The second Platonic development of the Socratic-Pythagorean portrait of the soul I mentioned above is its integration with
Plato's metaphysics: specifically, the doctrine of separately existing
Forms and the two-worlds view that the separate existence of
the Forms generates. This integration can be seen in the argument above, and in three other arguments in the *Phaedo*. From
the *Phaedo* on, the soul and the Forms will be closely associated in Plato's thought. One scholar, F. M. Cornford, described
the immortality of the soul and the theory of separate Forms
as the "two pillars" of Platonism. It is the soul that links the
intelligible world of the Forms with the world of phenomena
that we inhabit, and that provides an answer to the "greatest
difficulty" argument of the *Parmenides*, discussed in chapter 2.
Especially when it is separated from the body, but even when
embodied, the soul seeks to understand the Forms. Even when
embodied, the soul looks to the intelligible world as its proper
home. As the metaphysical picture of two worlds persists in later
dialogues, so does the conception of the soul as an intermediate
substance, whose natural home is the world of the Forms, but
which must be incarnated at intervals. Reincarnation, the legacy

of Pythagoreanism in Plato's thought, combined with the meta-physics of Forms, produces the idea that recollection must be of Forms, which the soul can perceive in its disincarnate state, after death and before its next birth. Recollection connects the soul with the concept of knowledge and with the Forms; it tells us that knowledge is of the Forms.

This combination of the theory of Forms with the doctrine of reincarnation has an effect on what I might call the "geography" of the afterlife. In the Socratic picture of the afterlife, as presented in the *Apology* and elaborated in the *Gorgias*, all souls of the dead go to Hades to be judged. Now the idea of a judgment after death is not something that Plato ever abandoned: it can be found in the *Republic*, the *Phaedrus*, and in the *Laws*, Plato's last work. But Plato could not place his Forms in Hades; the world of the Forms had to be the one inhabited by the celestial gods. Therefore, not all souls could descend into Hades after death. The *Phaedrus*, as we shall shortly see, places the Forms outside the rim of heaven. At the end of the *Republic*, in a passage known as the "myth of Er," souls who are judged are sent to one of two places: the just go to heaven; the unjust go beneath the earth. There they are rewarded and punished, respectively, for the lives they have led. This scheme is repeated in the *Phaedrus* and in the *Laws*.

The third point concerns the complexity of the soul. Up to and including the *Phaedo*, we have been dealing with a unitary conception of the soul. The basic contrast has been between soul and body. Psychological states like pleasure and pain are (or at least are caused by) states of the body. The soul is what exists when intelligence has been separated from these bodily states. Emotions, such as fear, are treated as states of the intellect, as judgments. It is the intellect that is immortal. In the *Republic*, however, a very important change occurs. As I mentioned in chapter 1, Plato divides the soul into three parts, assigning to each part a different psychological function. One function of reason is to direct the lower parts of the soul (a second function is to know the truth, reality), the function of spirit is to support reason, and the function of appetite is to see that one's basic physical needs are met. When the lower parts of the soul are dominant, the rational part of the soul cannot perform either of its functions. The good of the entire soul is not served in this case. On the other hand, when these three parts are in their proper order, the soul is just, and reason can pursue the truth. Plato summarizes this tripartite picture of the soul at the end of Book IX of the *Republic* by drawing an analogy between the soul and a figure made up, first, of a many-headed beast, representing the appetites; next, a lion, representing spirit; and finally, a human being, representing reason. To say that injustice pays, says Socrates, is to say that it is right to feed the many-headed beast and allow it to control the human being, whereas to say that justice pays is to say that it is best to strengthen the human being and domesticate the beast, making an ally of the lion.

As with earlier developments in Plato's treatment of the soul, once this tripartite analysis of the soul is introduced, it is retained, in the *Phaedrus* and *Timaeus*. The *Phaedrus* in particular provides a memorable image of the soul as a chariot, with a charioteer (reason) guiding two winged horses (spirit and appetite) during a voyage to the highest regions of the universe, where the gods live. There it acquires direct knowledge of the Forms, but the horse that represents the appetites will not allow the chariot to remain in the upper realm: it pulls the whole soul downward. The soul loses its wings, and is embodied. Only by living the philosophical life through three successive thousand-year cycles can it regrow its wings. According to the *Phaedrus* myth, all three parts of the soul are immortal: the appetites in particular are needed to explain embodiment. The *Timaeus*, which was written after the *Phaedrus*, maintains that only the rational part of the soul is immortal; Timaeus explicitly refers to the spirited and appetitive portions of the soul as mortal. Plato seems to suggest this possibility in the *Republic* when he says, "to see the soul, as it is in truth, we must not study it as it is while it is maimed by its association with the body and other evils … but as it is in its pure state" (*R*. X, 611b–c). He draws out a comparison to the sea god Glaucus, whose real nature is hidden beneath seaweed, seashells, rocks, and other debris of the ocean; if we want to see his true nature, we must lift him out of the sea and hammer off all of the debris attached to him. Likewise, Socrates says that to see the true nature of the soul we have to lift it up out of the human life in which it is immersed and focus on its love of wisdom. Then, he says, "we'd see what its true nature is and be able to determine whether it has many parts or just one" (*R*. X, 612a). This at least suggests that the soul has a tripartite nature only when it is embodied; the disembodied soul might be the pure intellect, the soul as Socrates understood it to be. If that is the case, the *Republic* would seem to side with the *Timaeus* against the view of the *Phaedrus* that the whole soul is immortal.

Fourth, Plato's account of personal identity shows an advance over the Socratic-Pythagorean account. According to that account, it would appear that the soul simply was the person. The soul in the *Gorgias* retains the identity it had in life, and the Pythagorean account seems to regard the reincarnated soul as the same person it had been in a previous life. At the end of the *Republic*, however, in the myth of Er, Plato modifies this account somewhat. According to this story, attributed to a warrior named Er who died in combat and came back to life twelve days later, having been given a glimpse of the afterlife, the souls of the dead retain their identities from their previous lives throughout the thousand-year period of reward and punishment they experience after death. At the end of this period, however, they choose new lives: they take on new identities, and become new persons. The soul remains the same but the person changes. The soul forgets its past life and enters a new life, taking on an identity that it will retain throughout the next thousand-year cycle. The soul is immortal, but the person is not.

The final development in Plato's view of the soul originates with an argument in the *Phaedrus* that occurs immediately before the myth of the chariot: all soul is immortal, because it is always in motion; it moves itself, whereas what is moved by another eventually ceases to move and thus ceases to live. Soul as self-mover is the source of all movement in other things; it cannot have a beginning, and so it cannot be destroyed. If a source of motion were destroyed, it could never get started again from nothing and nothing would begin to move. Without soul, everything would eventually come to a stop. But since this is not the case, as motion is everlasting, soul must also be everlasting: an eternally existing self-mover. This argument offers a new characterization and function for soul. This view of the soul as a self-mover is found again in the *Timaeus* and in Book X of the *Laws*; in all three places, it is connected to a cosmological function of the soul. Soul, that which moves itself, causes matter, body, which would otherwise be inert, motionless, to move. Plato seems to be talking in all these places about the force that moves the cosmos; in the *Timaeus* in particular, he refers to the "World-Soul." But as things are in the universe as a whole, so they must be in the individual: the soul of the individual must be a self-mover, and thus immortal, too. The ancestor of this conception of the soul as self-mover is the Socratic conception of the soul as a center of agency, and in particular moral agency; but the cosmic application and the proof of immortality are new in the *Phaedrus*.

As I have tried to show, the Platonic conception of the soul builds on the Socratic and develops naturally out of it, with the addition of the influence of Pythagoreanism. Though Plato's final account of the soul, as a tripartite, self-moving knower of the Forms, goes beyond its Socratic and Pythagorean origins, Plato retains the central features of the Socratic view: the immortality of the soul, the definition of death as separation of the soul from the body, the conception of the soul and body as distinct kinds of things, the idea that the soul is the center of agency, the view that the soul undergoes judgment after death, and the insistence that care of the soul should be our primary task. Plato also retains the

Pythagorean concept of reincarnation and the epistemological doctrine of recollection that he develops out of it. Plato's account of the soul is a synthesis of the Socratic and Pythagorean conceptions of the soul, as modified by his own metaphysical views.

# Aristotle

When we turn to Aristotle after considering the views of Plato, we need to remember two things. First, Plato's approach to the question of the soul, like his approach to other aspects of philosophy, is rich, informed by his metaphysics, and imaginative; he describes the life of the soul as a journey from its embodied existence to its home among the Forms and back again. I earlier described Plato as the poet of classical metaphysics and epistemology; it is the same with his view of the soul. Aristotle's approach is much more scientific and matter-of-fact than Plato's. As I noted in chapter 2, Aristotle is not only a great philosopher but also a great biologist, and his view of the soul reflects that fact. Second, the two philosophers' accounts of the soul are tailored to their respective metaphysics and epistemologies. Plato posited the soul as a bridge between separately existing Forms and their sensible participants. Aristotle, however, rejected the separate existence of the Forms. For Aristotle, form was not separate, but integrated within the complex particular. It might be the primary aspect of the particular, but it was an aspect of the particular for all that. Correspondingly, the task of reason was not, as it had been for Plato, to rise above the flux of the phenomenal world and discover the eternal, unchanging world of the Forms; it was, rather, to discern the form in the particular. The only true substances, thought Aristotle, were biological specimens (with one exception, the Unmoved Mover, which will be discussed in chapter 4), and biological specimens were combinations of form and matter. The form of these biological substances, Aristotle thought, was their soul.

Aristotle's primary work on the soul, *De Anima*, is a work both of philosophical psychology and of biology. In it, Aristotle gives a very broad, general account of the functions that distinguish various kinds of living beings; in his other biological works (which comprise about twenty percent of his surviving writings), he gives a much more fine-grained account of these kinds and how they differ from one another. What does it mean to say that Aristotle has a biological conception of the soul? To answer this question, we must remember that Aristotle was a *hylomorphist*: he regarded substances as combinations of matter and form. Aristotle, like Socrates before him, sought to understand things in terms of their definitions. Like Socrates, what he sought were "real" definitions: definitions of kinds of things, not just words. He thought that a proper definition stated the essence of a thing. Accordingly, in investigating soul, Aristotle sought to define it. When Aristotle gives his "official" definition of soul, in *De Anima*, he uses the language of matter and form, but he also uses the language of potentiality and actuality: "the soul must be a substance in the sense of the form of a natural body having life potentially within it. But substance is actuality, and thus the soul is the actuality of a body as above characterized" (*De An.* II.1 412b20–22). So the soul is the form, the actuality of a natural body. Correspondingly, the body is the matter, the potentiality, out of which the natural living being comes to be. What does this mean? As we saw in chapter 2, the actuality/potentiality distinction is a dynamic version of the form/matter distinction. What the form of a living being does is to actualize the potentiality contained in the matter. If we are to understand matter, we must understand it in relation to form. That is, we must understand it *teleologically*, in terms of its purpose, what we called in chapter 2 its final cause.

Aristotle sees the world as composed of living beings in an inanimate environment. But the contrast between the inanimate and the animate is not a sharp one. For Aristotle, the animate is made from the inanimate. The most basic components of the universe are the opposites: hot and cold, wet and dry. These combine to form the elements: fire (hot and dry), air (warm and moist), water (cold and wet), and earth (cold and dry). The elements in various combinations form the materials from which the body is made: bone is a certain ratio of elements, blood another, and so on. And these materials combine to form, first, bodily organs, then systems of organs (think of the skeletal system, or the digestive system), and finally the whole body, which is matter for the soul, and thus for the whole being. Each lower stage of development, from opposites to elements, from elements to more and more complex things, exists for the sake of the higher stage of development. Ultimately, the lower levels or stages exist, collectively, for the sake of the soul.

What separates the living beings from the inanimate background is that the living beings *do things*. In *De Anima*, he describes six basic functions that living beings perform:

1) Nutrition and reproduction
2) Locomotion
3) Desire
4) Perception
5) Imagination
6) Reason

Obviously, not all living beings do all of these things. Plants nourish and reproduce themselves, but they do not perform any of the other functions on the list (at least not according to Aristotle). Animals perceive things, and with perception comes desire. (The basic desire is for food.) Most animals move about as well. Some animals have the ability to remember things—bees remember where the flowers are and can direct other members of their hive to them—and memory is based on imagination. Aristotle says that those animals with memory are capable of learning. Finally, there is reason, which Aristotle thinks is restricted to human beings.

Reason in turn is divided into two powers: a passive capacity to receive the intelligible form of objects, and an active power to recognize that form. These two powers are called, respectively, the passive intellect and the active intellect. So we have a hierarchy of natures—a hierarchy of souls—based on the number of faculties the various species possess.

To understand the relation between soul and body more clearly, consider a part of the body, such as the legs. Legs are clearly a material part of any animal that has them. We can study them as such: we can investigate their physical make-up, their shape and size, and so forth. But we understand legs best when we understand them in terms of their function, which is to enable the animal to get around. That is, we must understand them in terms of the form of the animal that has them. Granted, legs have to be made of certain material if they are to perform their function. Aristotle says that you can't make a saw out of wool or wood; similarly, you can't make legs out of water or even mud. But if we ask why legs have to be made out of material that has a certain strength and rigidity, we must refer to their function: they must support the body and enable it to move. We understand the matter of which a thing is composed by referring to its form; that is, by referring to the function it fulfills.

So Aristotle understands the soul as being related to the body as form is to matter. This is not an accidental relationship; it is an essential one. For all psychological functions (Aristotle thinks there is one exception, reason), the soul requires a body in which to function. Often there must be a quite specific part of the body associated with a particular activity. Aristotle would reject the Pythagorean/Platonic idea that a soul might transmigrate into the body of a member of a different species: the connection between body and soul is far too specific for that. The soul of a human being can only be embodied in the body of a human being; in fact, Aristotle seems to think that each soul must be embodied in one particular human being. I don't think Aristotle would know what to make of John Locke's celebrated puzzle of a prince and a cobbler waking up one morning in each other's body (if you don't know the Locke puzzle, think of *Freaky Friday*); I think he would declare such a situation to be impossible. For Aristotle, personal identity is the identity of body and soul in combination. This obviously rules out immortality: when the body dies, the soul ceases to function, and so can no longer exist. (Again, Aristotle makes an exception for reason.)

What applies to individual organs of the body applies to the living organism itself. Now you might object at this point that there aren't really two things here, but one: a natural living being that can be looked at from two perspectives: the perspective of the definition or the essence of the thing, or the perspective of the material from which it is made. But that is exactly Aristotle's point: form and matter, actuality and potentiality, are aspects of a single whole, for the most part inseparable from each other. Aristotle makes this point with an analogy between the relation between matter and form and the relation between a piece of wax and the imprint of a stamp on it: "we can dismiss as unnecessary the question whether the soul and the body are one: it is as though we were to ask whether the wax and its shape are one, or generally the matter of a thing and that of which it is the matter. Unity has many senses (as many as 'is' has) but the proper one is that of actuality" (*De An.* II.1 412b5–9).

If we examine things "from the bottom up," stressing the role of matter, it may look as though the matter is the only real component of the composite, that it accounts for the entire nature of the living being, that the form is something conceptual, mental, or maybe even a definition in the verbal sense only, but not real. But Aristotle insists that we look at things first and foremost "from the top down." The bones and muscles and nerves that make up a leg won't do so unless the leg is attached to a living body. As Aristotle says of an eye, an eye that is detached from the body and cannot see is an eye in name only. The same thing applies to a leg. Aristotle insists that the form of a living being figures in the actualization of its nature in three distinct ways. First of all, as we have seen, it is the nature of the living being, the formal cause of its being. Second, it is responsible for the growth and development of the living being. It provides the end state toward which the living being is striving. It gives the specifications that guide the living being's growth. This is what Aristotle called the final cause of a thing. Finally, it is the cause of the generation of the thing itself. Now, as I noted in chapter 1, Aristotle has a theory of generation that has come in for a great deal of criticism in recent years for favoring the role of the male parent over that of the female parent. Briefly, he believes that the male parent transmits the form of the living being to the offspring in the womb, while the female parent provides the matter. But before that controversy arose, Max Delbruck, a Nobel Prize-winning biophysicist, wrote an article in which he (half seriously) said that Aristotle should be awarded a posthumous Nobel Prize for the discovery of DNA. Aristotle may have been wrong about the details of reproduction, and especially the female role in it, but he was right about this: in reproduction, the form of the living being is transmitted from the parents to the offspring.

I would suggest that, despite Delbruck's partially tongue-in-cheek claim that Aristotle discovered DNA, it is precisely DNA that Aristotle lacks. He has the right idea: in reproduction, the form of the natural kind is transmitted from parents to offspring, but he doesn't have the right mechanism. He couldn't, since the discovery of DNA required powerful empirical techniques, involving the electron microscope, as well as advanced discoveries in biochemistry that were not developed until almost 2400 years after he lived. But, if I may speculate, I think, if Aristotle were alive today and if he had been brought up to date on modern genetics, he would have embraced the idea that DNA was the carrier of the information vital to the reproduction, growth, and development of the individual living being; that is, that it was the carrier of the individual's form.

To return from the realm of speculation to Aristotle's actual text. In chapter 2, I gave an account of Aristotle's epistemology, which was based on a hierarchy of faculties outlined in *Metaph.* I.1–2: first perception, then memory, then experience, and finally reason. The account Aristotle gives of our cognitive faculties in *De Anima* closely parallels that account. In dealing with Aristotle's psychology in the remainder of this section, I want to bring out some of the relevant features of that account that bear on the account in *Metaph.* I. I am going to focus on the three faculties that explain cognition: sensation, imagination, and reason. But first let me remind you of Aristotle's general strategy for explaining the relation between body and soul. In general, where there is a psychological function, there is a corresponding physiological process. Or it might be better to say, there is but one event or series of events, which is understood in two different ways. As Aristotle says with regard to the emotion of anger, "a physicist would define an affection of soul differently from a dialectician; the latter would define e.g. anger as the appetite for returning pain for pain, or something like that, while the former would define it as a boiling of the blood … surrounding the heart. The one assigns the material conditions, the other the form or account" (*De An.* I.1 403a29–403b2).

How does this apply to the sequence of sensation, imagination, and reason? Let's consider sensation first. All animals possess it. The most basic sense is touch, which all animals have; higher animals possess forms of sensation such as sight and hearing, which permit the sensation of objects at a distance. Now there are two aspects to sensation, as Aristotle describes it. Sensation is, first, a *physical* process whereby particular parts of the body are modified by objects in its environment; Aristotle spends a good deal of time in *De Anima* talking about this physiological process as applied to each of the senses. Second, sensation is a process of *cognition*, in which information about those objects is conveyed to the soul. To give an example, sight is the modification of the eye by the medium of light, a modification caused by color. Color is what Aristotle calls a "special sensible," by which he means a property that only one sense can perceive. Only sight can perceive color. But there are also "common sensibles" perceived by more than one sense, such as shape and motion (or its absence), which can be perceived by touch as well as sight. So when I perceive a yellow ball, sitting at rest on the floor, my organs of sight, my eyes, are being modified by a physical process to take on the "sensible form" of the ball, without the matter. That is the physical definition of sight.

But sight is also the actualization of a capacity to become *aware of* the existence of an external object, in this case the yellow ball. The primary objects of awareness are the particular sensory qualities of that object: its color, shape, and motion. Only secondarily is it the awareness of an object: in this case the ball. Sensation of this incidental object of perception is fallible, but the sensation of the primary, particular object of perception, the color I perceive, is infallible. When my sense of sight perceives color, or when the sense of touch perceives roughness, or when the sense of hearing perceives sound, I perceive, not representations of the external world, but real properties of things in that world. When I perceive all of the sensible properties of an object and assemble them together in my mind, I perceive what Aristotle calls the "sensible form" of the object. Aristotle has a causal theory of perception: the soul is modified by a causal relation to the object. But what this causal relation brings about is a connection between the soul and the external world. Aristotle is a *direct* realist. In this respect, he differs from the Stoics and Epicureans, who are indirect or *representative* realists. There is, for him, no set of representations or images intervening between the external world and the mind to obscure that world; nothing stands between me and objects outside my mind. I see those objects, that world, directly. There is no "problem" of the external world, no possibility of skepticism, for Aristotle.

Now how are these two aspects of sensation—the physiological and the cognitive—related? Aristotle's answer seems to be that they offer two definitions of one and the same process, one definition stressing the material aspect, the other the formal. The physical modification of the eye just *is* the cognition of color in an external object. So far, the analysis of cognition in terms of matter and form, potentiality and actuality, seems to hold. When we get to the analysis of imagination, however, things become problematic. Aristotle defines imagination by indicating what it is: the power by which we are able to produce a mental image, but also by indicating what it is *not*. Imagination is not perception, for imagination occurs in dreams when our sensory faculties are inactive. Sensation is found in all animals, but imagination only in some. Sensations are always true, but imagination is generally false. Because our imaginings are generally false, imagination cannot be identified with knowledge or intelligence. Nor is it the same as opinion: some of the lower animals possess imagination, but only humans possess belief, and opinion involves belief. "Imagination is therefore neither any one of the states enumerated, nor compounded out of them" (*De An.* III.3, 428b8–9).

Let me illustrate Aristotle's points with a rather non-Aristotelian example. Though I am sitting in my office working on this book, and though I perceive myself to be doing so, I can easily imagine myself somewhere else: in a deck chair on a cruise ship, say, or on the beach in Hawaii. I can form this imaginative image only because I have had mental images of the various components of my image, formed by sensation, but it is clear to my senses that I am not at present either on a cruise ship or in Hawaii. Nor do I *believe* that I am at present in those states I imagine; to the extent that these images might suggest the contrary to me, they are *false*, and I know it. I do not for one minute think that I am anywhere other than in my study, but my imagination can place me elsewhere. (My imagination can, however, be a source of action: it can create a desire to be, say, on a cruise ship or in Hawaii, and this desire can be the basis of action, such as buying a ticket. Imagination can also, however, be idle daydreaming.)

But if imagination is not sensation (though it is impossible without sensation), not reason, and not opinion or belief, what is it? Imagination is the psychological power of voluntarily producing mental images, which are drawn from sensory images. Aristotle suggests that the power of imagination resides in the organs of sense, but later thinkers developed the idea of imagination, *phantasia*, "fancy," as a separate faculty. But if imagination is a separate faculty, where is it located? How are images produced, and where are they stored? Apart from the brief reference to the organs of sense, Aristotle does not offer a clue in *De Anima*. Our mental life in general he thought was seated in the heart (not the brain), so imagination may be located there. But Aristotle's analysis of imagination is exclusively cognitive—it is philosophical, epistemological: imagination is distinguished from sensation, from reason, and from belief. He does not describe the *physiology* of imagination. This analysis marks a transition from the largely physiological analysis of perception to the purely cognitive analysis of reason. But here is the most important aspect of imagination, for Aristotle: imagination is *necessary* for reason: Aristotle insists that we do not think without a mental image. (This contradicts Plato's view that, in the higher regions of thought at least, thought proceeds without images.)

When we come to reason, the detachment of the psychological from the physical is complete. You will recall, perhaps, that Aristotle in the *Ethics* had divided reason into three kinds: theoretical, practical, and productive, and that he had declared that the life of theoretical reason was the happiest life. Here he explains the operation of reason differently, cutting across the above divisions. The account of reason Aristotle offers in *De Anima* III, chapters 4–5 is one of the most abstract, difficult to interpret, and controversial in all of Aristotle. It is the passage in *De Anima* where Aristotle comes closest to embracing Plato's dualism. In order to explain this passage, we need to understand the problem Aristotle faced. Reason, for Aristotle, is the power whereby we understand what is real. But what is real? The intelligible form or essence of each object. In order for this cognition to exist, reason must know the form of each thing just as it is in itself. Reason must be "unmixed," as Aristotle states. If rational cognition were to take place by means of a bodily organ, as is the case with perception, the cognition would be affected by the matter that makes up that organ, and the cognition would no longer be of intelligible form *just as it is in itself*, but only of intelligible form *as perceived by a certain physical organ*. It would not be infallible cognition of what is real. This is not an acceptable result for Aristotle. Reason therefore must be an activity of the soul that is independent of any bodily organ. To put this matter in a different way, reason must know reality in the way Plato's soul knows reality when detached from the body. Plato has no trouble explaining this, for in his thought reality and the soul are made for each other. The soul is an immaterial substance and it knows immaterial Forms. Aristotle requires a similar explanation, but it does not fit well with his hylomorphism.

There are two aspects to reason: a passive and an active. The passive aspect or cognitive power is discussed in III.4, the active in III.5. It is important to remember that these two powers work together to produce knowledge. Intellect, for Aristotle, is a combination of actuality (the active intellect) and potentiality (the passive intellect), just as objects in nature are combinations of actuality and potentiality, matter and form. Consider first the passive intellect. This is the part of the soul that receives the intelligible form of the known object. This passive intellect cannot be made of some matter, for the reason stated above; it must therefore be pure potentiality. That is, it must be nothing at all before it thinks. The passive intellect is said to be like "a tablet on which as yet nothing actually stands written" (an idea later developed by John Locke in his idea of the mind as a blank tablet, a *tabula rasa*), but we must keep in mind that the passive intellect is not found in any matter.

What is it then that activates, actualizes, the pure potentiality of the passive intellect? It is the active intellect, discussed in III.5. What Aristotle says about this active intellect is extremely condensed and figurative: "And in fact thought, as we have described it, is what it is by virtue of *becoming* all things, while there is another which is what it is by virtue of *making* all things: this is a sort of positive state like light, for in a sense light makes potential colors into actual colors" (*De An.* 430a14–17; my italics). The active intellect is like light, but what does that mean? It must mean that it projects onto the blank tablet of the passive intellect the intelligible form of the object of knowledge, just as light makes it possible for the sense of sight to function. (Think of a movie projector, projecting images on a blank screen.) And what does it mean to say that the active intellect "makes all things?" It does not mean that the forms imprinted on the passive intellect are constructed out of whole cloth, that they have no counterpart in the external world. The work of the active intellect is to abstract the intelligible form of objects in that world; it is to reproduce in the passive intellect the *real* structure of the world, not to construct an *ideal* structure for the objects of sensation. Nor is it merely to abstract an *image* of that intelligible form, for then the question might arise whether that image corresponded to external reality; rather, it produces knowledge of the form *itself*. As light makes the sensible quality of color itself available to the eye, so the active intellect, which is like light, makes the intelligible form of objects available to the passive intellect.

Aristotle insists that the intellect has no bodily organ. This view seems open to the obvious objection that the mind is located in the brain, as Plato thought. Aristotle would surely have to revise his view of the intellect if he were alive today. I also think that Aristotle's account of reason runs counter to the general tenor of his philosophy of the soul, according to which each function of the soul is the actualization of the potentiality of some bodily organ or system of organs. I do not think that Aristotle is making a simple mistake in physiology, however. Rather, as I said, he is attempting to explain the fact that the mind understands reality just as it is. If the intellect were connected with some organ, it would be limited by that connection, and the claim that the mind could know form just as it is in itself would be problematic. This would theoretically open the door to an objection which was actually developed by later skeptics. We know the appearance of water, Sextus Empiricus stated, but not what water is in its essence. This result would not have been acceptable to Aristotle; he wanted to know the essence of things. Accordingly, he insisted that cognition was untainted by the interference of a bodily organ. It is not clear what he should say in response to this objection. Perhaps he should just bite the bullet and admit that intellect can only know reality as processed by the body (in this case the brain). He does say, after all, that reason operates on the sensible form of objects, and we receive the sensible form through perception, which requires a bodily organ. Or perhaps he should argue that the soul knows reality just as it is *despite* the fact that reason is housed in a bodily organ.

The fact that the intellect has no bodily organ opens the possibility of immortality for at least one portion of the soul. Just as Plato had stated in the *Timaeus* that the lower parts of the soul were mortal because they were housed in the chest and belly and essentially connected to the functions of the organs of those regions, Aristotle insists that most parts of the soul—nutrition and reproduction, sensation, imagination, and locomotion—must be mortal. But the intellect can exist separately from the body, and is thus immortal—or at least the active intellect is: "When separated it is alone just what it is, and this alone is immortal and eternal (we do not remember because, while this is impassive, passive thought is perishable) and without this nothing thinks" (*De An.* 430a22–25; with corrections). As is the case with the rest of this passage, this claim that the active intellect is immortal is perplexing and controversial. To begin, if the criterion for immortality is supposed to be independence of a bodily organ, it is not clear why the passive intellect as well as the active cannot be immortal, especially as it is related to the active intellect as matter to form. Further, it is difficult to see how the soul in its immortality can preserve the individual qualities of the person, and in fact Aristotle states that it does not (at least in the case of memory). So the active intellect is immortal, but its immortality does not seem to be anything like personal immortality. The perceptions of the individual are not immortal; nor is the individual's storehouse of images, his or her memory. The active intellect, when separated from the passive intellect, doesn't even have anything to impose its forms upon. What is immortal in the person would seem to be something like cosmic reason.

Aristotle's theory of the soul is an attempt to combine a naturalistic understanding of the soul as the source of life and of functions such as nutrition and reproduction, desire, and locomotion with functions that are more cognitive: perception, imagination, and reason. It may be that this combination is impossible to achieve within a single account. It may be that these two kinds of explanation—naturalistic and epistemological—just belong to different areas of inquiry and cannot be reconciled with each other. Even today specialists in neuroscience, cognitive science, and the philosophy of mind struggle to find an account of the cognitive powers of the mind that "maps onto" the brain. There is, in addition, a problem that Aristotle shares with Plato. For Aristotle, the soul is a form, the form of the body. It is not a separately existing Platonic Form, but it is a form nonetheless. Forms, like Platonic souls, are non-material; they are not bodies, and in fact are defined in contrast to bodies. Both Plato and Aristotle insist that souls act on bodies; in particular, they move the body with which they are connected. But how is this possible? How can what is not physical act on what is? How can what is not a body act on a body? This is a question that his successors, the Epicureans and the Stoics, answered with a resounding, "It can't. Only a body can act on another body. The soul must be material."

# Epicureanism and Stoicism

Though the Stoic and Epicurean philosophers are materialists, they are not materialists of the same sort: the Epicureans are more extreme materialists than the Stoics. Their materialism extends to their concepts of soul. Neither accepts the existence of the soul as a non-material entity. Does this mean that they reject the soul altogether? Not at all. Rather, they think of the soul as a material part of the being that has it. The challenge for ancient material-ism was to explain the functions of the soul, and in particular the higher functions such as reason, without appeal to a distinct kind of immaterial thing, whether a substance such as the Platonic soul, or an aspect of the living being, the form of the body, as in the case of Aristotle.

## Epicureanism

As we also saw in chapter 2, Democritus was the chief archi-tect of ancient atomism. The remaining fragments of Democri-tus' philosophy do not tell us much about his theory of the soul, though. Nor do the surviving texts of Epicurus. Fortunately, we have Lucretius' epic poem *On the Nature of Things*. It is Lucretius' testimony that I'll be concerned with when I discuss the Epicu-rean view of the soul. According to Lucretius, the soul is a complex entity, composed of four elements: breath, heat, air, and a nameless fourth element. The first three elements are included to explain the obvious features of a living body that are lacking in a corpse: corpses don't breathe, they lose the air they need to breathe, and they are cool to the touch, showing that they have lost heat. The fourth element is needed to explain all of the other functions of the soul, including perception. (Clearly, it is the nameless fourth element that does all of the "heavy lifting" in this theory of the soul.) The soul consists of these four elements in combination; none of them in isolation will suffice. The atoms that make up the soul are round and extremely fine; they communicate sensation through the body almost instantly. Lucretius distinguishes between two parts of the soul: the mind, *animus*, which is located in the chest and is the source of the emotions, as well as awareness, thought, and action; and the spirit, *anima*, which is spread throughout the body and is the source of sensation and transmitter of the commands of the mind to the rest of the body. In other words, when the sense organs perceive a lion, the spirit transmits that information to the mind, which interprets the lion as dangerous; the mind then formulates an appropriate plan of action, for instance to run away, and the spirit transmits that plan to the legs, which respond appropriately.

As in the theory of sensation and perception (see chapter 2), Epicurus does seem to take an *emergentist* approach to mental properties. The four kinds of atoms combine to form a complex structure, the soul. The soul then generates the properties we think of as most characteristic of the mind: perception, memory, belief, and knowledge. These emergent properties aren't properties of the individual atoms; they are properties of the complex structure the mind, which is, however, completely composed of those atoms. Just as a building such as a house has properties that are not the properties of the individual pieces of lumber, tile, etc. from which the house is made, so the mind has properties that are not properties of the individual atoms of which *it* is made. Yet for all that, Epicurus thinks, the house is composed of nothing over and above those individual pieces of lumber and the mind is composed of nothing over and above the atoms that form the soul. Epicurus, in other words, rejects Aristotle's idea that the soul, the "form" of the body, is something in itself, over and above the body it animates. Even more so, he rejects the idea that the soul is a separable substance, as Plato thought. The Epicureans are particularly concerned in their account of the soul to defend a central doctrine of their philosophy: that "death is nothing to us." We saw the reason this doctrine is of central importance in chapter 1:

Epicurus regarded fear of death, and in particular punishment after death, as the chief source of human anxiety. The Epicurean conception of the soul rules out the possibility of survival, and thus of punishment after death. At death, the structure of the soul is dissolved and the soul is resolved into the individual atoms that compose it; these atoms are dispersed back into the cosmos, and the soul ceases to exist. This doctrine is so important to Epicureanism that Lucretius offers twenty-nine (!) arguments in Book III of *On the Nature of Things* designed to show that soul and body are inseparably joined and that the soul cannot survive the death of the body. Epicurus rejects immortality also, but he retains the idea, common to all ancient philosophers, that the soul is the animating principle of the body: its presence is what makes a body alive. The soul is in addition the source of personal identity: as long as the soul exists, the person exists. The soul is also the cause of bodily motion, which is a problem both for dualists such as Plato and hylomorphists such as Aristotle; the soul can cause bodily motion simply because it is a part of the body. It can exert physical force over other parts of the body because it is itself a physical object. This is perhaps the greatest advantage of materialist theories of the mind over other theories.

But how, exactly, does the soul cause motion? Here is one possibility, which the Epicureans do *not* accept. Suppose the soul is simply a physical body like any other, formed by causal forces and acting in accordance with those forces and its own distinct structure. Imagine the soul, using the analogy of a bowling ball. Force is applied to the ball; it rolls down the lane and knocks down some pins. There is nothing in this example that is not explicable by the laws of physics. In this situation, however, it does not make sense to ascribe *responsibility* to the ball. True, the ball knocked down the pins, but only because just the right amount of force was applied to it. The analogy does not bring out the fact that the soul is an *agent*. Imagine, however, that the bowling ball has eyes, and can see the pins at the end of the alley. Imagine further that it moves on its own down the alley, having first *decided* to try to knock down the pins. *Now* we have a good analogy for human agency. If the motion of the bowling ball were fully determined by outside forces, the Epicureans think—if the world were deterministic—there would be no such thing as agency. For agency to be possible, there must be a gap in the causal sequence of events into which the soul can insert itself. This gap in the causal sequence is provided by the swerve. You will recall that Epicurus thought that atoms swerved occasionally from their downward course, striking other atoms and in the process building up the complex objects we perceive with our senses. Without the swerve there could be no agency. The swerve is what makes it possible for the soul to act freely, intentionally. This is where Epicurus' version of atomism differs from Democritus' version. In Democritus there is no swerve. The universe is completely determined by causal forces. Therefore, the Epicureans think, there could be no freedom. It was as much to explain the possibility of freedom as to explain the possibility of combination of atoms that the Epicureans introduced the swerve. There is, however, a large gap in the reasoning of the Epicureans on this topic; they don't explain, at least in the documents we possess, how the soul makes use of the indeterminacy in the causal sequence of events to act. There must be some power of the mind, some feature of that nameless fourth element, perhaps, that is able to exploit the indeterminacy of the universe in order to act on it. Otherwise, there would be no agency, only randomness or chance. Unfortunately, the Epicureans don't tell us what this power is. They are clear about one thing, however: in order for the soul to have freedom to act, there must be indeterminism in the causal sequence of events in the universe. There must be the swerve.

## Stoicism

For the Epicureans, causal determinism and freedom are *incompatible*. The Stoics deny this, as they deny other features of the

Epicurean view of the soul. To see some of the oppositions between Stoic and Epicurean psychology, let's begin with the disagreement between them on the composition of the soul. The Stoics were not atomists, of course; they accepted the traditional view that everything was made of a combination of elements: earth, water, air, and fire. The soul is made of *pneuma*, a combination of two elements: fire and air. The fire is not ordinary fire, but the "designing fire" (explained in chapter 2) that shapes events throughout the cosmos. The soul is thus a kind of breath. This is a view that goes back to Homer; it is the oldest concept of the soul in ancient thought. Air, of course, is the source of life itself, whereas the Stoics associate fire with the idea of rationality, for reasons we'll see in the next chapter. As the four elements in the Epicurean concept of the soul explained breathing, bodily warmth, and the elements of our mental life, so *pneuma* in the Stoic conception explains both how we live and how we think. The problem faced, or perhaps it would be better to say *not* faced, by the Stoics is the same as that faced, or *not* faced, by the atomists: how can a material substance have mental properties? How can the sage, who is perfectly rational, have a mental life at all? What is it about *pneuma* that makes it intelligent? It is tempting to think that this identification of the soul with two material elements must be metaphorical, but the Stoics take their materialism seriously. As with the Epicureans, we lack the texts we need to get from this materialistic view of the soul to the sophisticated analysis the Stoics offer of moral psychology. Unlike the Epicureans, who thought that the soul was dissolved at death and ceased to exist, the Stoics held that the soul, at least in the case of the sage, was immortal—it lasted as long as the cosmos lasted.

As we saw in chapter 1, the Stoics disagreed with the Epicureans on the end or goal of life. According to the Epicureans, the end or goal of life was pleasure, which they saw individuals pursuing from birth. This was called the "cradle argument." The Stoics denied this. They held that what every being sought from birth was to survive and to fulfill its own nature, to become a fully developed instance of the kind of being it is programmed to be. The Stoic understanding of the goal of life was thus *teleological* from the start. Two aspects of this goal in the case of human beings, which the Stoics called *oikeiôsis* or "affinity," were self-love and love for others. The Stoics thought that goodwill toward others was natural in humans. Human infants began to develop in a way that was proper or congenial to them from the start: it was this, and not pleasure, that they sought. At a certain point in their childhood, however, children developed the power of reason. From this point on, the aim of life for the Stoics was to realize one's nature as a rational being, to put reason, which they called the *hêgemonikon*, the "ruling element" of the soul, in charge. This meant developing virtue, which they regarded as the only good. You will recall from chapter 1 that the Stoics rejected the complex accounts of virtue put forward by Plato and Aristotle and reverted to the Socratic view that virtue was knowledge. They were *intellectualists* about virtue and the good life. They saw the appetites and emotions, not as separate elements in the soul, but as twisted or misinformed rational judgments, opinions or beliefs, which they aimed to avoid entirely. The moral development of the soul consisted in the replacement of the false opinions of the ordinary person with the true judgments, the knowledge, of the sage. Connected to reason were the five senses, which provide information to the ruling part. Reason stands in judgment over the various sensory images that present themselves to it, and the various emotions they produce, determining which are true representations of nature or reality. There are two additional parts of the soul, according to the Stoics: the reproductive part and voice. They describe the reproductive part in terms of "spermatic principles," literally seeds, by which the male parent transforms matter in the female parent's womb into a human being. (Here, as in their account of the teleological nature of human life and in fact of life in general, the Stoics seem to be following Aristotle's account.) It is not clear why the Stoics made voice, or speech, a separate part of the soul. Perhaps their point was to distinguish the inner workings of the soul, from its appetites and emotions to the deliverances of reason, from their outward expression in speech. These various parts of the soul—the senses, reproduction, and speech—are seen as connected to the ruling part like the tentacles of an octopus or the web of a spider.

As the Stoics differ from the Epicureans about the material nature of the soul and the analysis of moral properties, so they differ, fundamentally, on the nature of freedom. Modern discussions of freedom of the will describe three main positions. Two of these positions are based on the idea that freedom requires indeterminacy in the causal structure of the universe, that freedom is *incompatible* with determinism. The first of these, libertarianism (not to be confused with the political view of the same name), holds that there is such indeterminacy, and that we are capable of initiating new sequences of events by acts of our will. This is essentially the position held by the Epicureans. The second position holds that there is no such indeterminacy, and that therefore there are no spontaneous acts of will, and thus no freedom and no moral responsibility. This view, known as "hard determinism," was not popular in ancient philosophy. The third view disagrees with the basic premise of the first two, that causal indeterminacy is required for freedom. It holds that the universe is causally determined, but that for all that there is freedom and moral responsibility. Because it holds that freedom and responsibility coexist with a determinist universe, this view is known as *compatibilism*, or "soft determinism." The Stoics were compatibilists. For compatibilists, the key distinction that allows for freedom is the fact that some of the causal determinants of events are actions, things we have chosen to do, whereas others are events that happen to us. Our actions and our choices are free, and we are responsible for them, even if they are caused by our desires and beliefs, because these desires and beliefs are *ours*. On the other hand, things that happen to us independently of our own choices are not free. As an example, consider driving a car. Suppose, for example, that there is a sale on at a store I have never visited before on the other side of the city, and an ad in the newspaper says that they have an item I particularly want. I then decide to drive my car to the store. Everything I do to get the car from my home to the store is part of a causal sequence: I check my mirrors, press the accelerator, then the brake, signal my intention to turn, and so on. My actions in getting to the store are determined, and so was my choice to go to the store; but the point, for the compatibilist, is that they are determined by conditions internal to my own mind. Contrast this with something that happens on my trip that is not part of my own design—I get a flat tire, say, or my GPS malfunctions and directs me to the wrong location. These events are just as causally determined as my intentional actions, but they differ in that my choices play no role in them. True, I may have decided at some point to get a few more miles out of my old tires, or I may have decided when I got into the car to trust the GPS, but I did not desire, or choose, or will to have a flat tire or get lost. Philosophers have debated for centuries whether this distinction between internal and external actions is significant, as compatibilists claim them to be. If it is granted that my desires and choices are themselves determined, and that, given those choices, it was inevitable that I should attempt to go to my chosen location, how is my action free? How can I be held morally responsible for my choices if they are ultimately determined by causal factors that I don't control? It is often suggested that a person acts freely in a given situation, and is morally responsible for his or her action, if it is true of that person that he or she "could have done otherwise" in that situation. For one who denies that every event in the universe is causally determined, such as the Epicureans, this is fairly straightforward: one did $x$, but one might have done $y$, and if one had done $y$ the history of the cosmos would have been, if only in one tiny respect, different. Given that the universe is completely causally determined according to the Stoics, this notion of "could have done otherwise" is very difficult to understand. In what sense could an agent have done or chosen otherwise than he or she acted or chose, if all of our actions and choices are determined by previous actions or events? Isn't the fact that some causes are internal to me whereas others are external just an arbitrary distinction? This is what worried the Epicureans, and it worries other critics of the Stoics as well.

One aspect of Stoic compatibilism is not typically found in modern compatibilism. The Stoics thought that, when one sets out for the store, one's actions are conditioned by two desires, not one: not just to get to the store and buy the item on sale, but to keep one's mind in accordance with nature. Let us say that this latter desire is a "second order" desire, whereas the former is a "first order" desire. A first order desire is a desire to obtain something like a sale item at the store: typically, something in the world other than a desire. A second order desire, on the other hand, is a desire that is concerned with other, first order desires, specifically, the desire to have my first order desires conform to nature. Now there is one respect in which this second order desire is no freer than a first order desire: everyone desires to live the good life, the good life is a life of tranquility, and the only way to attain tranquility is to have one's first order desires conform to nature. I can never lead a good life if I am constantly at war, psychologically, with the way the world is. That means accepting a flat tire or GPS malfunction as something nature throws our way, as something that is not "up to us." Therefore, since I desire to live the good life, to be happy, it follows that I must desire that my first order desires conform to nature. But though this desire is not free in the sense of being one among several options, it is free in another sense: it is precisely the life one would choose to live if one had perfect knowledge of the future. It is a life free from psychic conflict, free from false belief and the distortion of the emotions. It is the life I *would* choose if there were several options. It is the perfectly rational life, the life of the sage. And the Stoics claim that only the sage is free.

According to the Stoics, I cannot change the way the world is. What I can work on, however, is my attitude toward the events I experience. Nor can I change the desires that I have right at this moment. I can, however, respond to the way the world responds to those desires by learning to conform my desires to the way the world is. This is the way of the sage. The sage is one who has learned not to endorse, rationally, every desire that occurs to him or her. The sage is one who has learned not to *assent* to attractive but misleading enticements. If my experience in the past has led repeatedly to my getting lost, I can learn not to trust my GPS. If the result of my assenting to desires in response to newspaper ads has been that my house is cluttered with useless objects I have purchased, I can learn not to assent in the future when I have those desires, and perhaps I can learn not to form such desires in the first place. That would be how one moves in the direction of sagehood.

Is this view consistent? The Stoics took pride in the internal consistency of their system. Their doctrine of free will is connected to their doctrine of the sage, which is connected to their doctrine of gripping impressions and assent. There is, however, an ancient objection to the Stoic position, called the "Lazy Argument." Suppose I am ill, and I wonder whether I should go to the doctor. I reason as follows: whether or not I will recover from my illness is something that is already determined. If it is determined that I will recover, I will do so whether or not I go to the doctor. If, on the other hand, it is determined that I will not recover, then once again it will not matter whether I go to the doctor. Therefore, I will not go to the doctor. Generalizing from this case, it will do no good to do anything, if everything is determined. Analogously, I will not strive to become a sage, because it is impossible to modify my desires. Whether I shall become a sage is already determined, so I shall do nothing to change the way I am. Chrysippus responded to this argument by saying that whether I went to the doctor and whether I recovered were not independent of each other. Going to the doctor may be essential to my recovery; it may be a crucial causal determinant in the process. In this case, going to the doctor and recovering are "co-fated"—if it is fated that I should recover, it is also fated that I go to the doctor. Likewise, I can become like a sage only by altering my desires. The end is "co-fated" with the means. This is what makes the study of philosophy essential: it shows the way to sagehood and the good life.

The Stoics and Epicureans disagreed about several things, including the nature of freedom, the composition of the soul, and its immortality. They disagreed about whether the cosmos was causally determinate, and therefore they disagreed about the nature of freedom. Though they disagreed about specifics, however, they shared two generic agreements: they agreed that the soul was material and that its will was free. In taking the soul to be material, they disagreed with their predecessors, Socrates, Plato, and Aristotle. The immaterialist conception of the soul never really explained how it was possible for the soul and the body to interact. This was the major advantage of the materialist conceptions of the soul found in Epicureanism and Stoicism. On the other hand, these two philosophies never managed to make it clear how a purely material being could possess the higher cognitive properties of the soul, especially those involving intentionality. These problems continue to plague the philosophy of the mind today.

# 4
# God and the cosmos

*It is right for me, gentlemen, to defend myself first against the first lying accusations made against me [by] my first accusers ... They got hold of most of you from childhood, persuaded you and accused me quite falsely, saying that there is a man called Socrates, a wise man, a student of all things in the sky and below the earth ... Those who spread that rumor, gentlemen, are my dangerous accusers, for their hearers believe that those who study these things do not even believe in the gods.*

(Plato's *Apology*)

## Socrates

In this final chapter, I want to examine a fundamental concern of the philosophers and schools we have studied so far: the existence and nature of God or the gods and their role in ordering the universe. Every one of the philosophers and schools we have studied in this book professed belief in the gods or God. In the case of the Epicureans, critics have suspected that they were merely paying lip service to traditional belief, perhaps to avoid the kind of prosecution that brought about the death of Socrates. (I doubt this; had the Athenians wanted to prosecute Epicurus for impiety, they could have found plenty of reasons for that in his unorthodox beliefs about the gods and their relations with humans.) I want to distinguish two philosophical paths to theology: an ethical path and a naturalistic one. The ethical approach begins with the idea that the gods are good and attempts to see what follows from that. The naturalistic approach begins with the idea of order in nature and attempts to discover what can be known about the gods from that. The former approach is basically deductive: it argues *from* the existence and goodness of the gods *to* various conclusions about the world-order. The latter is basically inductive: it argues *from* certain facts of nature *to* the existence and nature of the gods. Socrates is, I think, the founder of the ethical approach to theology. He rejected the naturalistic approach, which is the one taken by most of his predecessors in philosophy, the Presocratics.

What Socrates disavowed is any concern with the philosophical study of nature, in particular the investigation of things in the heavens and beneath the earth. Socrates followed the ethical approach exclusively. In the *Apology*, in response to the charge of his "first accusers" that he investigated things "in the sky and below the earth," a charge made vivid by Aristophanes' portrait of him in the *Clouds*, where he first enters suspended high above the stage, a form of entrance usually reserved for gods, Socrates says he knows nothing of such matters, and he asks the jurors to testify whether any of them has ever heard him discuss such matters at all. "I do not speak in contempt of such knowledge, if someone is wise in these things," he says, "but gentlemen, I have no part in it" (*Ap.* 19c). Xenophon, our other main source of information about Socrates, goes further: he says that Socrates thought that people who were concerned with these questions were foolish. "Human minds cannot discover these secrets, inasmuch as those who claim most confidently to pronounce upon them do not hold the same theories, but disagree with each other just like lunatics" (Xenophon, *Mem.* I.1). In so doing he turned his back on over a century of philosophical speculation about nature that had largely defined philosophy before he came on the scene. Why did he do so? Perhaps he just wasn't interested in the subject. If Xenophon's testimony is accurate, he thought such knowledge beyond the reach of humans. Yet he apparently thought knowledge of the first principles of ethics beyond the reach of humans too, and that didn't stop him from seeking it.

Plato in the *Phaedo* offers another explanation of Socrates' lack of interest in cosmological inquiry and speculation about nature in general, one that, on the face of it, is somewhat at odds with the blanket disclaimers of the *Apology* and *Memorabilia*. At the start of the passage that culminates in his final argument for the immortality of the soul, discussed in chapter 3, Plato's Socrates offers an account of his previous investigations into coming into being and ceasing to be. According to this account, Socrates *had been*, while young, very interested in natural philosophy, but he had become disillusioned with the kinds of explanation he had found in it. He had been momentarily excited by what he heard concerning Anaxagoras' Mind, but that promise had proved empty. Socrates could find no one to enlighten him on the subject of Mind and teleological explanation, and so he developed the theory of Forms as a second-best kind of explanation of change. The Forms are introduced, it should be noted, not as part of a teleological explanation, for Socrates has given up on that, but as a different kind of cause: we call them, redundantly and not very informatively, "formal causes." Much later in Plato's career, the Forms would play a central role in just the kind of teleological explanation that Socrates here abandons.

This passage in the *Phaedo* has been referred to as Socrates' "autobiography." Interpreters have differed, however, as to its historical basis. It is tempting to see in Socrates' account of his disillusionment with natural philosophy an explanation of his turn to ethical inquiry. It is hard, however, to reconcile it with the claim of Socrates in the *Apology* that he had *never* discussed such matters with anyone. It may be, on the other hand, that Plato is putting his own experience with natural philosophy into Socrates' mouth. This is a puzzle, I think, that can't be solved, like others I have mentioned that generate the "paradox of Socrates." Whatever the historical reality, Plato's dialogues prior to the late *Timaeus* show little interest in the naturalistic approach to theology and cosmology. On the other hand, these dialogues show continuous interest in the goodness of the gods. Socrates looked to the gods as the repositories of the moral wisdom that he thought humans lacked; and, since he thought that virtue was this very wisdom, he thought the gods must be ideal moral agents, perfect exemplars of virtue.

If one comes to Plato's Socratic dialogues from reading Homer or Greek tragedy, one might well think that Socrates had picked the poorest candidates possible for the role of moral exemplars. In the Homeric poems and in Greek tragedy, it is humans such as Antigone and Hector and others like them who are the ethically admirable characters. When not providing comic relief, as they do on occasion in Homer, the gods are usually displayed as the originators of immoral actions or commands, and as underminers of human virtue. The gods as portrayed by the poets are capricious and moody: in Homer's *Odyssey*, Poseidon keeps Odysseus from returning home for ten years after the end of the Trojan War because he is angry with him. In the *Iliad*, Apollo rains arrows of disease and death among the Greek host for basically the same reason. In Euripides' play *Hippolytus*, Aphrodite brings about the ruin of young Hippolytus because he does not honor her. Cases could be multiplied. Socrates and Plato objected to this portrayal of the gods, and undertook to reform their image. This reform is hinted at in the *Apology*, where Socrates says that he believes in the gods "as none of my accusers do," and where he mentions the judgment of the soul by wise judges after death. That judgment, as we saw in chapter 3, is affirmed in the *Gorgias* and remains a part of Plato's thinking until the end of his life. We find evidence for Socrates' revisionist attitudes toward the gods in the *Euthyphro*, where he tells Euthyphro that he finds stories such as that of Zeus punishing his father Cronus, and Cronos in turn castrating his father Ouranos "hard to accept." The program of reform culminates in *Republic* II, where Plato undertakes an extensive critique of the theology of the poets. Plato's gods, unlike the gods of the poets, don't quarrel or, worse, do battle with each other. They are good, and are therefore not the cause of everything that happens, but only good things; they are unchanging and truthful.

Socrates had an important predecessor in his ethical critique of the poets, and in particular Homer: the Presocratic philosopher Xenophanes of Colophon (c. 570–c. 475). Xenophanes had two main criticisms of the poets: first, that Homer's gods commit every moral wrong recognized by humans, and, second, that they are plainly cast in the image of human beings. The Ethiopians depict their gods as black, the Thracians depict theirs as red-haired; if cattle and horses had the ability to draw, he complains, they would depict their gods as cows and horses. The truth is that there is "one God, greatest among gods and men, in no way similar to mortals in body or in thought; always he remains in the same place, moving not at all ... but without toil he shakes all things by the thought of his mind. All of him sees, all thinks, and all hears" (frs. 23–6). Clearly, Xenophanes' conception of God goes beyond anything in Homer and Hesiod. It also seems to go beyond the early books of the Hebrew Bible, where God is often portrayed in anthropomorphic terms. Xenophanes' use of the phrase "one God, greatest among gods and men" raises a question that is difficult to answer, not just in Xenophanes' case but in Greek philosophy in general: is he a monotheist? If so, he may be the first true monotheist in the Western tradition. But what about that phrase "greatest among gods and men?" Doesn't that mean that Xenophanes is really a polytheist, with one head god and a bevy of lesser ones? Or does he mean that there is only one *real* God, the mover of the cosmos, and a number of lesser divinities who do various other things, much as the Abrahamic scriptures speak of God and angels? The issue of monotheism vs. polytheism does not seem to have concerned the ancient philosophers in the way that it concerned theologians in the Abrahamic religions (Judaism, Christianity, and Islam). The problem of interpreting the precise significance of Xenophanes' words extends to his statements about God's nature. On the one hand, he says that "God shakes all things with the thought of his mind," and "all of him thinks," phrases that suggest that Xenophanes' God is a pure mind. On the other hand, he says that God is "in no way similar to mortals in body or in thought," and that he remains in one place. It is clear that Xenophanes' God *has* a mind; it is less clear that God *is* a mind. (Aristotle complained that Xenophanes "made nothing clear." I think it is fair to say that the revolutionary idea of a monotheistic, purely mental God is present in Xenophanes' thought, but that it is not unambiguously expressed.)

As far as Plato is concerned, Socrates is entirely innocent of cosmology. It is a surprise, then, to turn to Xenophon's *Memorabilia* and find Socrates putting forward a teleological argument for the existence of God. The teleological argument, perhaps better known as the argument from design, in general goes something like this:

1) The cosmos, or some portion of it, shows signs of organization.
2) This organization cannot be explained as the result of accident.
3) Therefore, it must be the result of design.
4) Design requires a designer.
5) Therefore, the organization of the cosmos is proof of the existence of a designer or designers, which would be God or the gods.

Socrates offers three examples of organization that must be explained in terms of design: our sense organs, our instincts concerning reproduction, and our intelligence (which Socrates thinks must be shared by other things in the cosmos). He thinks that these examples of design show not only that the gods exist, but also that they care for us. In addition, he argues that our erect posture, our hands, and our sexuality (unlike other animals, who only have sex when they are "in season," we are able to enjoy sex at any time) also show that the gods care for us. Further, the gods make us aware of them, which leads to our worship of them. With our god-given minds we can acquire intelligence. Finally, the gods enable us to see into the future, via portents of various kinds and divination. This is the argument as presented in *Mem.* I.4. Later, in IV.3, he returns to the topic, but in an argument that is different in form. Here it is assumed that the gods exist; Socrates concentrates on showing that they have satisfied our needs. Some of the examples he raises are borrowed from the earlier argument, but some are new. The gods provide sunshine so that we can use our vision; darkness at night so that we can rest; earth so that crops may grow and satisfy our hunger; water to aid the crops in growing; fire as a defense against cold and darkness; the seasons to moderate the effects of cold and heat; animals for our use; senses (particularly sight) so that we may perceive beauty; and above all mind, which is our most godlike trait. In short, virtually everything in the universe, beginning with our own bodies, is proof of the fact that the gods exist and that they care for us.

We today are skeptical of the argument from design; the theory of evolution has shown that many features of human existence and the existence of other beings that appear to be the result of design can be explained instead as the result of evolution. But in Socrates' day the theory of evolution did not exist in a credible form. In its historical context, this argument does not look as bad as it might today. But now we are faced with a problem. Which portrait of Socrates is historically accurate: Plato's or Xenophon's? Was Socrates innocent of any account of cosmic teleology, as Plato argues? Or is he the author of the argument from design, as Xenophon states? It seems impossible to tell. All we can say for certain is that this argument for the existence of the gods, based on design in nature, was attributed to Socrates by one of the two authors who wrote most extensively about him. Either the argument is Socrates' and belongs to the fifth century BCE, or it is Xenophon's and belongs to the fourth.

# Plato

Plato attempted to combine the Socratic concern for moral theology with the concern of earlier philosophers, such as Xenophanes, with a philosophical study of nature. Plato turned to cosmology late in life, in the *Timaeus*, in which he presents a full-blown cosmology, an account of the nature of the universe. The *Timaeus* is the first complete essay on cosmology we possess from the ancient world, and its influence in antiquity was enormous, despite the fact that it is written in an elevated style that makes it difficult to understand. Plato's cosmology is developed from three basic principles: the Forms, which serve as paradigms—standards or models—from which the cosmos is constructed; the Receptacle, the matter out of which the cosmos comes to be; and the Demiurge (the name literally means "Craftsman" or "Artisan"), the divine originator of the cosmos. Though Plato admits the existence of numerous lesser deities, to whom in fact he assigns the task of creating human beings, the Demiurge is clearly his primary deity. When Plato lays out his cosmology, the first question he asks is:

> Why did he who framed this whole universe of becoming frame it? Let us state the reason why. He was good, and one who is good can never be jealous of anything. And so, being free of jealousy, he wanted everything to become as much like himself as was possible … the god wanted everything to be good and nothing to be bad so far as that was possible,

and so he took over all that was visible—not at rest but in discordant and disorderly motion—and brought it from a state of disorder to one of order, because he believed that order was in every way better than disorder.

(*Ti.* 29d–30a)

Plato's assumption is that the Demiurge is good. He derives the goodness of the cosmos from this initial assumption. At this point, a remark about the word "cosmos" may be in order. I use this word more or less synonymously with "universe," though some philosophers, in particular the Epicureans, speak of multiple cosmoi in the universe. We are familiar today with the term, from well-known television series as well as other sources. The Greek word *kosmos*, however, carries an implication that may be missing, or extremely curtailed, in modern discussions. To say that the universe is a *kosmos* is to say that it is ordered—and not only that, but that it is ordered in a beautiful, elegant way. The oldest use of the verb *kosmeo* is "to set an army in array, to marshal it." This suggests that, if the universe is a cosmos, there must be someone who put it in order, as a general orders an army. For the Greeks, this order had an aesthetic dimension. The order of the universe was something beautiful to behold. Even today, when people describe the universe as a cosmos, they imply that the universe is ordered, and that science can make sense of the order: it is not a pile of unintelligible junk.

In terms of the distinction I drew above between a deductive, ethical approach and an inductive, cosmological approach to theology, the *Timaeus* is definitely in the deductive camp. It begins with the assumption that the Demiurge is good, and derives its account of the cosmos from that. The cosmology of the *Timaeus* is a teleological theory, and without the initial assumption of the Demiurge's goodness Plato could not explain the features of the cosmos teleologically, in terms of their suitability to achieving a good end. The *Timaeus* offers just the kind of cosmological theory Socrates had accused Anaxagoras in the *Phaedo* of promising but not producing. Though there are a couple of references to the Demiurge in the *Republic*, for all practical purposes, the Demiurge is a novel element in Plato's cosmology in the *Timaeus*.

This is not the case with the second element in Plato's cosmological scheme, the Forms. The Forms of the *Timaeus* are essentially the same entities as the Forms of the *Phaedo, Symposium, Republic,* and *Phaedrus,* now put to a cosmological use. Like any artisan, the Demiurge must look to a pattern, a blueprint if you will, as a model in designing the cosmos. The recurrence of the Forms in the *Timaeus* indicates that Plato did not abandon the theory in light of the critique of the *Parmenides.* Plato even presents a brief argument for the existence of the Forms in the *Timaeus,* to which I alluded in chapter 2. Is there any such thing as Fire "by itself," existing in an intelligible realm, Timaeus asks, or are the things that we see the only things that exist? He responds that, if understanding and true opinion are distinct, and if instruction differs from persuasion, then separate Forms exist, ungenerated and indestructible, invisible, never entering into anything else, known by understanding and not by the senses. Since understanding and true opinion clearly are distinct, then the Forms must exist. Whatever intelligibility the created world possesses is due to the Forms and the Demiurge. In creating the cosmos, the Demiurge implants images of the Forms in the phenomenal world. As I mentioned above, it may help to think of the Forms in this context, admittedly anachronistically, as blueprints, and to think of the whole set of Forms as one huge blueprint, an intelligible plan, for the construction of the cosmos. Because the Demiurge is good, as the quotation above indicates, he makes the cosmos as good, as much like himself, as possible. Now every good artisan looks to the perfect, uncreated model, rather than a created model in creating his product. The Demiurge of course has no created models to look to, since he is creating the world, but in any case he would look to the perfect model in his creative activity. That is, the Demiurge looks to the Forms as models, standards, or patterns, in creating the cosmos.

The final element in Plato's cosmological scheme is the Receptacle. The Demiurge embodies images of these Forms in a plastic material, which he calls the Receptacle, or nurse, of Becoming. Like the Demiurge, the Receptacle is a novel element in Plato's account. Up to the *Timaeus*, Plato had thought that there were two kinds of things in the universe: unchanging, intelligible Forms and changing phenomena. The Receptacle is a third kind of thing. As I mentioned above, Plato describes it as a "plastic material" out of which the cosmos is created; alternatively, he calls it space, the medium in which the Demiurge reflects the Forms. If the Forms are strictly eternal features of Plato's cosmology, and if the Demiurge is a bridge between that eternal world and the created one, the Receptacle is an everlasting foundation of the created world. It does not exist *in* time; rather, time is the result of the Demiurge's creative activity in the Receptacle. Plato describes the Receptacle as containing traces of the elements in disorderly motion before the Demiurge begins his creative work (see the passage quoted on page 145–6). Plato says it is apprehended by a kind of "bastard reasoning"; perhaps because, unlike the proper objects of reason, the Forms, it has no definite intelligible nature of its own. The Receptacle is almost defined by its lack of an intelligible nature: it is in its essence nothing in particular.

The Receptacle limits what the Demiurge can do in creating the world. One may wonder why this is so, especially if we treat the Receptacle as if it were just empty space. I think, though, that this fact alone explains part of the limitation placed on the Demiurge. The Forms are not spatio-temporal entities; but the copies the Demiurge makes of them are. These copies are not duplicates of the Forms, but images in three dimensions. These images must exist in space and time. If the Demiurge wants to create a world in which cats exist, he must embody the Form of Cat in the Receptacle. But even though the Form of Cat is a purely intelligible object, an embodiment of that Form must contain the kind of matter out of which cats are made. In terms of the traditional four elements of ancient cosmology—earth, water, air, and fire—cats are mostly earth; the Demiurge can't embody the Form of Cat in air, or fire, or even water. So the Demiurge is limited in what he can make. Plato describes the creation of the cosmos as the interaction between two factors: reason and necessity. By necessity, Plato doesn't mean mathematical or rational necessity (that would be reason) but the force that limits the activity of reason, that prevents it from perfectly embodying rationality in the created order. That necessity is the Receptacle. In addition to the problem of imaging non-spatial, intelligible objects in space, however, there is the additional factor that space, for Plato, isn't just empty. Before creation, as I have noted, there are traces of the elements in disorderly motion in the Receptacle. What the Demiurge does is to *order* these disorderly traces; he doesn't create them. Space is a plastic material, but it is not infinitely plastic. It resists the efforts of the Demiurge to create images of the Forms in it.

The created universe is called by Timaeus the world of "Becoming." Becoming is related to Being as copy is to original, as phenomenal things are related to intelligible Forms. This division of reality into two kinds—the eternal Forms and their temporally limited images—originated when Plato first separated the Forms, in the *Phaedo*; Plato used the terms "Being" and "Becoming" in the *Republic* when he distinguished knowledge from opinion. Before the *Timaeus*, Plato had accepted the *fact* that there were two kinds of things in the cosmos: Forms and their phenomenal images; the *Timaeus* explains the *reason* for the existence of those two kinds. In Plato's mind, it is the existence of Becoming that requires an explanation: Being does not. The existence of Becoming is explained by adding the Demiurge and the Receptacle to the world of the Forms. Given that there should exist a vast expanse of nearly empty space, with just some traces of elements in disorderly motion, it was inevitable, due to the goodness of the

Demiurge, that he should attempt to bring as much order to the Receptacle as possible. That meant forming the plastic material of the Receptacle in light of the model of the Forms. Without the Receptacle and the Demiurge, there would have been no cosmos, only the Forms.

There is a controversy, beginning in ancient times, almost as soon as Plato wrote the *Timaeus*, as to how literally we are to understand the story it tells. For the *Timaeus*, if interpreted literally, is a creationist account of the cosmos. It is not quite right to say that for Plato the world is created *in* time; time is something that comes to be with the creation of the cosmos. Still, there is a sense of "before" according to which, for Plato, before the Demiurge began to act, there was only disorder in the universe, and after which order, including temporal order, existed. Several of Plato's followers in antiquity theorized that Plato meant the creation of the cosmos by the Demiurge to be a figurative expression of a quite different fact: the ongoing creative activity of intelligence in a cosmos that had no beginning. Others, including Aristotle, treated the account of the *Timaeus* literally. In this chapter, I follow the literal sense of the text and assume that the *Timaeus* is a creationist cosmology, but the reader should be aware that another interpretation of the dialogue is possible.

We can deal briefly with most of the details of Plato's account. The cosmos came to be; time came to be with the universe. Plato describes time, rather poetically, as a "moving image of eternity." The motions of the heavenly bodies divide time into intervals; the cosmos is a grand celestial clock. As it was to be as much like its creator as possible, the Demiurge implanted intelligence in it, and, because intelligence requires soul, he made a soul for it, which he called the World-Soul. The cosmos is unique. When the Demiurge has created the cosmos in its grandest outlines, he creates lesser divinities and gives to them the task of creating the mortal creatures of the cosmos, including humans. The souls of humans are equipped with sense perception, with love, mingled with pleasure and pain and with fear, spiritedness, and accompanying emotions. The result of the influx of data from the senses and the resulting emotions is that the new-born soul is in a state of turmoil until reason can restore order.

There is one feature of Plato's cosmology that I want to dwell on in a little more detail, however, and that is his theory of the elements. Plato accepted the traditional view that there were four basic "elements" of nature: earth, water, air, and fire. He did not regard them as genuine elements, though—an element is an absolutely basic building-block of creation, and these four "elements" were made of something more fundamental, more elementary: triangles. Plato's theory of the elements is a response to a problem encountered by the Pythagoreans. We saw in chapter 3 that Plato's account of the soul and his doctrine of Recollection were influenced by Pythagoreanism. The Pythagoreans influenced Plato in another matter as well. They had tried to construct a cosmology based on mathematical principles, specifically on numbers. They ran afoul of the fact that some of the numbers they encountered in constructing the cosmos were "irrational," however: they could not be reduced to a ratio between two whole numbers. The Pythagoreans had been shocked at the discovery that the world could not be explained in terms of combinations of rational numbers: they refused even to call the quantities, such as the square root of two and the square root of three, numbers. They called them instead "irrational magnitudes."

Plato dealt with this by placing the irrational numbers right in the elements to begin with. Plato made the four "elements" of traditional cosmology out of two basic triangles, which had irrational numbers as lengths of their sides. He then assembled these triangles into three dimensional figures. One kind of right triangle, with the dimensions 1, 1, $\sqrt{2}$, formed the cube, which Plato said was the elemental shape of the earth; another right triangle, with the dimensions 1, $\sqrt{3}$, 2, formed the basis of the tetrahedron (four-sided pyramid), octahedron (eight-sided "double pyramid"), and icosahedron (twenty-sided figure); these were the elemental shapes of fire, air, and water. These latter three elements can transform into each other by breaking down into their component triangles and recombining to form new solid shapes. There are exactly five regular solid geometrical shapes: these four figures and a fifth figure, the twelve-sided dodecahedron, which looks like a soccer ball and which Plato said resembles the shape of the cosmos as a whole. They are known as the "Platonic solids" (see figure 2).

The mathematician Theaetetus, a member of Plato's Academy, developed the account of the geometry of these solids. Plato decided to construct the universe out of them. These elementary shapes are Plato's answer to Democritus' atoms. Unlike Democritus' atoms, they have a mathematical nature, and they are reducible, in the end, to just two triangles. By "mathematizing" the elements, and thus space, Plato ensures that the cosmos has a

**Figure 2:** The five Platonic solids

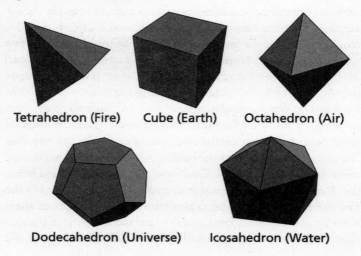

Tetrahedron (Fire)   Cube (Earth)   Octahedron (Air)

Dodecahedron (Universe)   Icosahedron (Water)

rational structure, despite limitations of the Receptacle, "all the way down."

Plato's cosmology is without question original; but its originality consists in part in its synthesis of several disparate elements from Presocratic philosophy. As I have just noted, his theory of matter is indebted to the Pythagorean project of explaining the cosmos mathematically and to the atomic theory of Democritus. It is also indebted to the work of various Presocratic philosophers who over time developed the theory of the four elements. That theory originated with Thales, the first philosopher in the Western tradition, in the sixth century, who claimed enigmatically that everything was water, and culminated in the philosophy of Empedocles in the fifth century. Plato borrows something from all three accounts of matter, which had existed as rival accounts in the works of his predecessors, but in so doing he creates an account of matter combining aspects of those rival theories that goes beyond any of them. The same can be said of the Demiurge. The origin of the Demiurge may be found in Xenophanes' conception of one God who shakes everything in the universe with his mind, but it also has an ancestor in Anaxagoras' Mind. Yet neither Xenophanes nor Anaxagoras had developed the teleological aspect of the creative activity of God as Plato does; this was just Socrates' complaint against Anaxagoras in the *Phaedo*. The benevolence of the Demiurge explains his purpose in creating the cosmos, and ensures that everything in it is ordered for the good, as Socrates had sought.

There is one component of Plato's cosmological scheme that is not developed from the theories of his Presocratic predecessors, of course, and that is his theory of Forms. This aspect alone would mark the cosmology of the *Timaeus* as distinctively Platonic. What the *Timaeus* does is to take this theory, which is presented in the *Phaedo* not as a teleological explanation of things, but as an alternative, "second-best" explanation, and make it a part of a teleological explanation. Socrates had said in the *Phaedo* that he would

gladly learn of such an explanation from someone; Timaeus—
and thus Plato—is that someone. The cosmology of the *Timaeus*,
with its "two-tiered" theory of reality, does, however, provide
an answer to a problem from Presocratic philosophy. Plato saw
Heraclitus, perhaps unfairly, as a philosopher of perpetual change;
in the *Theaetetus*, he had argued that, if this Heraclitean view
of nature as never-ending flux were correct, knowledge would
be impossible. Aristotle says that Plato accepted the Heraclitean
characterization of the phenomenal world, but posited the intelligible world of the Forms to explain the existence of knowledge.
Parmenides, finding change unintelligible, had argued that reality, being, must be a single eternal unmoving sphere-like entity.
Plato had portrayed a very young Socrates in the *Parmenides* as
arguing that, though only the Forms were eternal, unchangeable, and intelligible, the sensible world could possess a measure
of that intelligibility by participating in those Forms. The world
of Becoming is not for Plato a purely Heraclitean world, despite
what Aristotle had said; it has a measure of intelligibility, due to
its participation in the Forms, which is brought about by the
goodness of the Demiurge. Thus, the Platonic cosmology recon-
ciles, to some degree, the extremes of Heraclitean perpetual
change and the Parmenidean timeless being via the benevolent
activity of the Demiurge.

Plato turns to theology for a final time in Book X of the *Laws*,
his last work. Here he is interested in proving three things about
the gods: that they exist, that they care for human beings, and that
they cannot be bribed by prayers and sacrifices. Only the first of
these topics will concern us here. His opponents are atheists; he
does not name them, but he offers a brief account of their views.
They say that the heavenly bodies are just earth and stones, and
thus are incapable of caring for human beings. They claim that
the four elements—earth, water, air, and fire—exist by chance
and move at random, by virtue of their own nature. There is no
design in the universe; everything results from nature and chance.

The gods are just artificial constructs, legal fictions. There is no divine punishment of wrongdoers, and so no reason for people to obey the law, if they can get away with breaking it. Plato's response is that the soul is prior to the four elements and must have been created first. The soul is the cause of the motion of the elements; the soul itself is a self-mover, as we saw in chapter 3 that Plato had argued in the *Phaedrus*. The soul is the cause, not just of the physical motion of the elements, but of good and evil, beauty and ugliness, justice and injustice, and all the opposites. Plato distinguishes two kinds of soul: a soul that seeks beauty, goodness, and order, and its opposite, a soul that seeks evil, ugliness, and disorder. Looking at the universe, one can see that it is moved by a good soul or a number of souls, for the movement of the heavenly bodies is regular and orderly. The souls that move the heavens are gods. This argument combines two features usually considered separately. First, there is the argument that the universe must have a cause that sets it in motion, and that ultimately this must be a cause that moves itself. This borrows a premise from the cosmological argument for God's existence, which says that there must be a "first cause" of motion in the universe. Second, there is the premise that, since the universe must be moved by soul, the evidence of the universe shows that it is moved by a good soul or souls. This premise comes from the argument from design, discussed above in connection with Socrates.

Apart from this passage in the *Laws*, Plato is not interested in confronting atheism. His opponent is popular religion, whether in the person of Euthyphro or in the myths of Homer and Hesiod. Plato has a religion, and it is expressed symbolically in the Demiurge of the *Timaeus*. It is the religion of rationality, and its enemy is superstition. The undoubted maxim of Plato's world-view is that the world is ordered teleologically, in accordance with rational principles. This world-view has as a corollary the ethical principle that we, as rational beings, ought to strive to be as much like God as possible. Thus, Plato's religion is ethical throughout. From the earliest mention of the gods and the Forms in the *Euthyphro* to the creation story of the *Timaeus*, Plato's gods look to the Forms for the knowledge that guides their activities. Since Plato's gods, unlike Homer's, are not driven by their emotions, it would seem that their virtue is, as Socrates had said of human virtue, a matter of knowledge.

# Aristotle

If Plato's approach to cosmology and theology, following Socrates', was thoroughly ethical, Aristotle's was, as we might expect from previous chapters, naturalistic. Despite this fundamental difference in approach, Aristotle's theology resembles Plato's in certain respects. Both Aristotle's and Plato's accounts are teleological in nature, and both feature a single divine principle as the first cause of the motion of the cosmos. Aristotle's cosmology is based on the general principles of his philosophy. You will recall that Aristotle thought that the primary category, on which everything else depended, was substance, and that every substance was a combination of matter and form. In the case of a human being, for instance, the body was a complex system of organized matter, whereas the form, the soul, was the principle that organized that matter and caused it to perform actions characteristic of human beings. The soul was defined as the actuality of an organized body, whereas the matter or body of a human being was the set of potentialities or possibilities that the form actualized. In general, form was related to matter as actuality to potentiality. Aristotle also distinguished four "causes" or kinds of explanation: material, formal, moving (efficient), and final. Natural beings had forms that were organized teleologically, with an end in view. Motion or change took place for the sake of that end.

Aristotle used his conceptual scheme to explain the operation of the entire cosmos, literally from the ground up. He divided the cosmos into two regions: the sublunary region (literally, the region "beneath the moon") and the heavenly region. In the sublunary region, everything is composed of the four elements of earth, water, air, and fire. These in turn are composed of four opposite qualities: hot and cold, wet and dry. Earth is cold and dry, water is cold and wet, air is hot and wet, fire is hot and dry. Each of the elements has a natural place in the cosmos toward which its motion is directed. The cosmos has a center, toward which both earth and water naturally tend; Aristotle understood gravity to be the force that made these elements move naturally toward the center of the universe. Air and fire, on the other hand, tend by nature to move to the outer circumference of the sublunary world. Though the natural motion of each of the elements is in one direction only, the elements can move in other directions if force is applied. A rock can be thrown in the air, forced to move upward for a time before its natural tendency to move downward takes over.

In adopting the theory of the four elements, Aristotle follows the dominant tendency of the Presocratics, represented in its most mature form in Empedocles. In this respect, his theory of the sublunary realm resembles Plato's. While Plato made the entire cosmos from these four elements, however, Aristotle limits them to the sublunary realm. To explain the motion of the heavenly bodies, Aristotle posits a fifth element, the *aithêr*. His reasoning is that the sublunary elements move in one direction only, up or down in a straight line, but the heavens manifestly move around the earth in a circular motion. Therefore, they must be made of different stuff than are earthly bodies. The heavens are also, Aristotle thought, eternal. Therefore, the *aithêr* must be eternal. It has potential for motion, otherwise it would not move; but it cannot be created or destroyed.

For Aristotle, no body moves itself. Every motion of each body in the universe, whether in the sublunary or the heavenly world, is determined by the form of that body. It is the form of natural living bodies, their soul, that dictates their motion. Likewise in the case of the elements: fire moves up because that is its nature, its form. And likewise for heavenly bodies. Now what Aristotle says about the heavenly bodies is not as clear as it might be. It is not clear, in particular, whether Aristotle sees the heavenly bodies as intelligent beings, or whether he sees their motion as guided by intelligent beings that are not identical to them. In either case, however, it is the nature of each heavenly body to move in a circle. The form of each heavenly body is what causes it to move. But motion, for Aristotle, is the actualization of potentiality. Each heavenly body, at any given point on its circular orbit, has the potential to be at another point on its orbit—halfway around, for example. What causes the heavenly body to actualize the potential to move to that other point?

Aristotle has two answers to that question. The first answer is "the nature of the heavenly body itself." But the heavenly body in itself has only the *potential* to be in motion. What causes it to actualize that potential? The second answer is "the purpose that heavenly body is striving to achieve." The heavenly body, or its guiding intelligence, actualizes its potential because it wants to achieve some final state. What is that state? The heavenly body, by its perpetual circular motion, aims to imitate the perfect motionlessness of the Unmoved Mover. The Unmoved Mover has no unactualized potentiality; it is pure actuality. Now what, you may ask, could have that property in Aristotle's system? The answer is: pure thought. Recall that Aristotle said that the highest attribute of the soul was its active intellect. The active intellect, he believed, was pure thought, the thought that "makes all things," in that it extracts the forms of various substances from them and impresses them on the passive intellect. Our thought, the kind of thought we are familiar with, is actually the product of these two psychological traits. Our passive mind is a blank tablet; it is purely receptive. Our active intellect does all the work of thinking. But *our* active intellect is concerned with the forms of the things we experience. Its task is to enable us to "get around" in the world. The Unmoved Mover has no such practical concerns. Moreover, if its thought flitted from object to object continuously, as our thought does, it would be in some sense dependent on those objects for the content of its thought. Then it too would have some potentiality and it wouldn't be really "unmoved." Aristotle's solution to this problem is that the Unmoved Mover thinks continuously about the finest thing in the universe: itself. The Unmoved Mover is pure thought, thought thinking about pure thought. Our active intellect, at its very best, may fix its attention on the highest thing in the universe for a few minutes at a time; the Unmoved Mover thinks about itself continuously. Everything in the cosmos imitates this perfectly actualized substance. Even natural substances lower than human beings, substances that have no conscious thought of the Unmoved Mover, imitate the immortal perfection of the Unmoved Mover by trying to attain eternal life in the only way that they can: by reproducing themselves, by creating another being like themselves. Everything in the universe strives to achieve its own nature; but in so doing it also tries to attain the perfection of the Unmoved Mover.

Why is the Unmoved Mover a necessary part of Aristotle's system? Because, in Aristotle's physical system, actuality precedes potentiality. Matter of an appropriate kind, which is potentially human, can be made actually human only by the activity of form. Without a parent providing form, there would be no human being. Aristotle's answer to the question "Which came first, the chicken or the egg?" is "the chicken." Moreover, because Aristotle thought the universe was everlasting and uncreated, he thought there had always been members of the same species we see today. The theory of evolution, which puts potentiality before actuality, is the polar opposite of Aristotle's theory. Moreover, the ideal of perfection sought by things can't be merely a theoretical ideal, existing only in their minds. It has to be an actual ideal. Therefore, the Unmoved Mover must exist.

Aristotle was aware that the motion of the universe could not be described as a single, simple circle. Plato had been aware of the work of the astronomer Eudoxus, who was a member of the Academy, and had incorporated it in his *Timaeus*; Aristotle was also aware of the work of Callippus, a younger astronomer. Each of these astronomers had attempted to explain the various motions of the heavenly bodies, including the sun, moon, and planets, by positing a series of concentric spheres on which the bodies moved. Their systems were quite complex; moreover, they were purely mathematical models. Aristotle, in modifying their model to make it physically possible, had to introduce a number of additional spheres to counteract the motion of those Eudoxus and Callippus required. The result was that he needed fifty-five spheres to account for the motions of the heavenly bodies, plus one for the "fixed stars." Aristotle seems to think that each of these spheres required its own Mover, so that there would be fifty-five Unmoved Movers. On the other hand, he presents an argument for a single Unmoved Mover. There is one heaven, he says, and if there were many Movers they would have to be individuated by matter, which would give them potentiality. The first Mover must be one in formula and one in number, he concludes, and at the end of his discussion of the Unmoved Mover he quotes Homer as saying, "The rule of many is not good; one ruler let there be."

The question remains: if the Unmoved Mover engages only in contemplation about its own nature, how does it move the cosmos? Aristotle's answer is: by being a final cause. It cannot be a moving cause, because it is unmoved. It cannot be a material cause, because matter is potentiality and the Unmoved Mover has no potentiality. Neither is the Unmoved Mover the formal cause, or essence of the universe. The only possibility remaining is that it should be the final cause, the goal or purpose toward which everything in the universe strives. The whole universe, apart from the Unmoved Mover, is made up of entities that are combinations of matter and form, potentiality and actuality. As each entity strives to actualize itself, it also strives to be pure actuality. The Unmoved Mover, the only pure actuality in Aristotle's cosmology, is the necessary first principle that is the object of every other entity's movement. Though Aristotle makes his point in terms of his metaphysical categories of actuality and potentiality rather than in ethical terms, the Unmoved Mover resembles Plato's Form of the Good in being the ultimate object of desire of all beings in the universe.

There are at least three objections that could be raised to Aristotle's cosmology, apart from the obvious ones raised by modern science. The first, which must strike every reader, is that the Unmoved Mover looks rather self-absorbed. There it is, like its close relative, the man of theoretical reason, thinking constantly of one thing. But at least the theoretically wise human being thinks about something other than himself; ultimately, he thinks of the highest thing in the universe, which is the Unmoved Mover. But the Unmoved Mover thinks of the best thing in the universe too, and that is itself. It thinks of itself constantly, and never becomes bored. This may seem to be a somewhat facetious objection, but it has important implications for the governance of the universe. According to Aristotle, the Unmoved Mover cannot exercise providence: it cannot even know that the universe exists, let alone govern it. Aristotle's later followers had to modify his concept of the Unmoved Mover substantially to make it compatible with the God of the Abrahamic traditions (see pages 162–3).

The second objection is that the Unmoved Mover moves things by being a "final cause," an object of desire. But, one may object, in ordinary cases of final causation, it is not necessary for the final cause actually to exist in order to motivate the agent. Consider a carpenter, planning to build a house. Aristotle says that the formal cause of the house is the idea of the house, existing in the mind of the builder. But the final cause is the projected house, which does not exist until the carpenter actually builds it. Why can't the Unmoved Mover be an ideal of perfection, motivating everything in the universe to seek it, without actually existing in reality? Third, consider the nature of the Unmoved Mover: pure actuality. Aristotle's fundamental pairs of concepts—form and matter and actuality and potentiality—were designed to explain the nature of substances like ourselves, composites of both. Actuality is almost by definition the actuality of some potentiality. We saw that for Aristotle pure matter, pure potentiality, could not exist. Why suppose that pure actuality, not the actuality of some potentiality, could exist?

Despite these problems, Aristotle's theistic cosmology was immensely influential—not in the ancient world, where Plato's cosmology ruled the day, but in the medieval world where philosophers in all three Abrahamic traditions sought to reconcile Aristotle's theology with that of their religion. It was not because of the intuitive appeal of Aristotle's theology itself; in that respect, Platonism was a much better fit. Rather, it was Aristotle's success in explaining nature that led philosophers to adopt his theology. When the Aristotelian system of nature broke down, at the end of the Middle Ages and the beginning of the modern world, so did the appeal of Aristotelian theology. It remains influential, however, in the theology of the Catholic Church, where St. Thomas Aquinas, perhaps the greatest Aristotelian who ever lived, still has the status of theologian *par excellence*.

## ANCIENT PHILOSOPHICAL THEOLOGY AND THE ABRAHAMIC RELIGIONS

The parallels between the views of the ancient philosophies, and in particular Platonism, Aristotelianism, and Stoicism, and the God of the Abrahamic religions are obvious. So, however, are the differences. Plato's Demiurge resembles the God of the Book of Genesis in creating the cosmos with the end in view of making it as good as possible. According to the Abrahamic traditions, however—but perhaps not the text of Genesis itself—God creates the universe *ex nihilo*, out of nothing; the Demiurge creates it out of a pre-exist-ing, plastic material. The Demiurge is thus limited in what he can do; the Abrahamic God is unlimited. Also, the Demiurge does not create the Forms on the basis of which he creates the cosmos. They are independent of his mind and limit his thought. The God of the Abrahamic religions, on the other hand, is again unlimited. Finally, Plato gives the function of the daily governance of the cosmos to the World-Soul, whereas the Abrahamic God is both creator and governor of the world. Because his Demiurge is limited, Plato does not face the "Problem of Evil" that Abrahamic theologians do: he does not have to explain the presence of evil in a world governed by an all-powerful, all-knowing, benevolent God. Plato's Demiurge is benevolent, but neither all-powerful nor all-knowing.

Aristotle's Unmoved Mover differs from the Abrahamic God in three basic respects. It does not create the cosmos, for Aristotle's cosmos is uncreated. It does not know the cosmos, or any of the individuals within it, including ourselves; it only knows itself. Finally, it does not exercise governance over the world. Despite these facts, the medieval philosophers Moses ben Maimon (Maimonides), repre-senting Judaism, St. Thomas Aquinas, representing Christianity, and Ibn Rushd (Averroes) and Ibn Sina (Avicenna), representing Islam, took Aristotle's Unmoved Mover, rather than Plato's Demiurge, as their model for God. Despite the facts that the God of Stoicism was material, a designing fire, and that the cosmos in Stoic philosophy was without beginning or end, but at intervals consumed by fire and then reconstituted, the Stoic God had one feature that was congenial to the Abrahamic religions: it exercised providence over every event in the entire universe. None of the three traditions by themselves offers divine first principles that correspond precisely to the God of the Abrahamic traditions, but together they provide a philosophical foundation for Abrahamic theology.

## Stoicism and Epicureanism

In the last part of this chapter, I want to consider two ancient materialist conceptions of God: those of the *Stoics* and *Epicureans*. Now it is strange to modern ears to think of God or the gods as material, but Stoicism was guided by the principle that what acts on matter must itself be material. Since God creates and governs the cosmos, on their view, God must be material. The Epicureans had an even simpler view: to be is to be material; the gods exist; therefore, the gods are material. Both philosophies also maintain that the cosmos is material: there are no immaterial Platonic Forms or Aristotelian essences. Despite their agreement on these points, however, the Stoics and Epicureans had radically different conceptions of God and the cosmos.

## Stoicism

Let's consider first the views of the Stoics. The Stoic world consists of two parts: a passive, plastic material, motionless and formless, which resembles the Receptacle of Plato's *Timaeus*, and the moving cause that organizes this formless matter and imparts motion to it. This power is called God, but it is not the immaterial being of Anaxagoras, Plato, and Aristotle. It does not exist separately from the cosmos; rather, it is immanent in it. God is conceived as a body, on the grounds that nothing can act on a body except a body. Thus, matter and God are both bodies. This active body, which works on the plastic, passive matter, is also described as fire, but it is a special kind of fire, an intelligent, *designing* fire, as was explained in chapter 2. The Stoics are not unanimous about the nature of the active element: some sources say that it is not fire but *pneuma*, the material that makes up the soul. *Pneuma*, however, is composed of this designing fire plus air, so the designing fire is on all accounts at least an ingredient in the active force that makes everything happen in the universe.

One of the characteristics of this designing fire is that over time it gradually consumes more and more of the plastic material of the universe, until everything is finally burned up. This total consumption of the passive material by the active material produces what the Stoics called the "conflagration"; it is followed by a complete "reconstitution" of the world in its previous state. (Imagine an expansion of the universe, following the Big Bang, followed in turn by a return of the cosmos to its original state, and then by another repetition of the process.) Now the Stoics were complete determinists about the occurrence of events—they thought that each event was completely determined by a set of antecedent causes—so they had no alternative to regarding the reconstituted universe as an exact copy of the one that had been destroyed. This thinking led to a cosmic cycle, in which each conflagration was endlessly succeeded by an identical reconstitution. The events of the current world are conceived of as endlessly repeated: thousands of years from now, after the next conflagration, an exact duplicate of me will be writing an exact duplicate of this book for an exact duplicate of you to read. The fragments of Stoic writing that we have offer no explanation for this periodic consumption and reconstitution of the world. Perhaps they thought that, as it was the nature of fire, even a designing fire, to consume things by burning them, this must happen on a cosmic as well as a small scale. Moreover, the reconstitution of the cosmos is a problem: how does God accomplish it? Why does the cosmos not cease to exist when the plastic, passive material is consumed? How can a designing fire exist without fuel? The Stoics say the world would turn into flame or light at the moment of complete conflagration, but why does it not simply burn up? Perhaps it was because of questions such as these that some later Stoics did not accept the doctrine of conflagration and reconstitution. Some, a minority, held that the universe was uncreated and eternal.

The remarkable feature of Stoic cosmology, the feature that sets it apart from earlier theories, is the fact that the active causal power in the cosmos is both fire—though admittedly a special kind of fire—and an intelligent, divine being. Whether we believe in God or not, we are used to thinking of God in the manner of Plato and Aristotle, as an immaterial being, and we are apt to find the juxtaposition of materiality and intelligence strange. Given the fact that the Stoics are materialists, God *must* be a material being; but why do they identify God with an elemental being, rather than one with a complex physiology? Granted, of the elements, fire is the one that is most obviously active, and it is cosmic activity that the Stoics wanted to explain. Granted further that fire might be thought of as the material element closest to an immaterial nature—we might classify it under the category of energy rather than matter—still, there is much here that is unexplained. Whether this is due to the fragmentary nature of our evidence is something we can't know. In the remainder of the chapter, I'll focus on the intelligence of the divine cause, rather than its materiality.

The Stoic God, like Plato's, aims at producing the finest cosmos possible. Due to the resistance of the Receptacle, Plato's Demiurge cannot completely determine the course of the universe: accidents happen, and things don't always go according to plan. The Stoic God, on the other hand, exerts complete control over the events of the cosmos. Perhaps this is because the passive material of the Stoic cosmos, unlike Plato's Receptacle, exerts no contrary force to reason; perhaps it is because the Stoic God is an indwelling principle of the cosmos, rather than an initial artisan creator; perhaps other factors are involved. However that may be, the Stoic God exercises control over the cosmos down to the finest detail. Since God intends for the universe to be as good as possible, and since nothing can impede its intention, the universe *is* the best possible, and everything in it is ordered in such a way as is in the best interest of the whole.

This understanding of God's activity has a ripple effect throughout Stoic philosophy, from its ethics to its epistemology and psychology. I discussed earlier the sage's acceptance of events, when those events proved inevitable. Now it becomes clear that for the Stoics every event is inevitable. When the Stoics say that they want to live in accordance with nature, what they mean is that they want to live in acceptance of the inevitable unfolding of events in the cosmos. I spoke earlier of the Stoic acceptance of fate; now it can be seen that fate is not some blind result of the interaction of unintelligent physical forces, but the result of an infinitely wise and benevolent God's foresight: in other words, providence. The sage, who is the person who understands this, sees not just that he or she must accept what happens as inevitable; he or she must understand it as good, indeed as the best thing that could happen. To become a sage is to develop the ability to experience not resignation but joy in the face of events. The wisdom of the sage is just his or her ability to understand that the universe is ordered in the best possible way. The freedom of the sage is the sage's ability to de-center his or her self from his or her particular life and to identify with the purpose of the cosmos as a whole. It is no wonder that the sage is extremely rare, if not non-existent.

Stoic cosmology and theology have precursors in Presocratic philosophy, as do the cosmologies and theologies of Plato and Aristotle. The identification of fire and divine reason has its origin in Heraclitus. Heraclitus was seen by Plato and Aristotle as a philosopher of flux, of motion; but through the constant motion Heraclitus saw the *logos*, reason, as the organizing force of the cosmos. This "one thing," this unifying factor in the cosmos, "was willing and unwilling to be called Zeus." He claimed that the universe as a whole was an "ever-living fire," kindling and going out in various parts. The idea of a cosmic cycle is even older than Heraclitus: it goes back to Anaximander, one of the earliest philosophers, who thought that the elements emerged from the opposites and disintegrated again into them "according to necessity," in a perpetually recurring pattern.

## Epicureanism

Finally, I turn to the second variety of materialism in ancient philosophy, that of Epicurus. In one respect, the Stoics were more consistent materialists than the Epicureans. The Stoics said that all that *existed* was matter; while the Epicureans allowed that void, empty space, had an existential status equal to that of matter. The Stoics, however, allowed several kinds of non-material entities, such as place, time, void, and "sayables" (speech), a kind of quasi-reality.

These things did not exist in the world of matter and the designing
fire, and only matter really existed; but they were something rather
than nothing. This difference is rather small and, perhaps, termino-
logical; it centers on what we mean when we say that something
exists. Other differences between the two philosophies are more
significant. For the Stoics, matter, the passive element in the
cosmos, was a single continuous entity of finite dimensions, like
Plato's Receptacle, existing in infinite empty space, void. The
cosmos was unique—there was only one cosmos—and it was full,
a plenum, with no empty space inside it. For the Epicureans, on
the other hand, there were many cosmoi, existing in different
portions of the void, and each cosmos was composed of atoms
intermingled with void. Matter, for the Epicureans, came in
imperceptible, indivisible particles, not in a single visible mass.

The major difference between the Stoic and the Epicurean
cosmologies, however, lay in the causal role they assigned to
God or the gods in forming the cosmos. The Epicureans in fact
gave the gods *no* role in forming or administering their various
cosmoi. They accepted the existence of the gods—at least they
said they did—and they regarded the gods, like everything else,
as made of atoms. They understood the gods as intelligent beings,
human in form, completely happy, imperishable, existing somewhere in the universe, but not enmeshed, like the Stoic God,
in the matter of this particular cosmos. We know the gods exist
because films sent off from them strike our minds, in particular
when we are dreaming, producing a universal acknowledgment
of them in every culture, a "preconception," as Epicurus called
it. We perceive the gods just as we perceive other persons and
objects. Because Epicurus held that all perceptions were true, he
held that our perceptions of the gods are true, at least as far as
their existence and nature is concerned. When it comes to the
activity of the gods, however, most humans are quite mistaken.
We think of them as seeking to punish us for our sins, but the
gods, being eternally blessed, could not care less about human

conduct. We can't be punished after death because our souls dissipate after death; but, even if we were immortal, the gods have more important things to do than to be concerned with evaluating our conduct. Rather, they spend time in company with each other, living lives of perfect pleasure. Their existence is that to which the Epicurean philosopher can only aspire. Fear of the gods, even more than fear of physical pain, is what makes humans unhappy. If they have the correct—that is the Epicurean—view of the gods, then they can be relieved of fear and attain tranquility.

The Epicurean portrait of the order of the universe could not be more different from the Stoic portrait. Whereas for the Stoics God orders every aspect of the cosmos, for the Epicureans the cosmos is literally the result of chance: random combinations of atoms that swerve from their downward paths and collide with each other. There is organization, which results from these elementary collisions, but there is no design. The purposelessness of the Epicurean universe is supposed to produce exactly the same result as the complete providence of the Stoic universe: it is supposed to produce tranquility in the mind of the person who believes in it. Just as the Stoic philosophy is an integrated picture—the sage, who knows that God has ordered everything for the best, is able to live in a deterministic universe with perfect freedom, secure in the knowledge that freedom is limited to one's attitudes, not to one's actions—so is the Epicurean philosophy: the Epicurean philosopher, aware that nothing in the universe is ordered by God, lives in an indeterminate, purposeless universe where one is utterly free to act. The Pyrrhonian skeptic, looking at this vast disharmony between these two positions, and seeing no rational basis for choice between them, advocates the suspension of judgment on all questions of cosmology and theology. The remarkable thing about this state of affairs is that each of the three philosophers, the Stoic, the Epicurean, and the Pyrrhonian skeptic, claims to be able to bring about the same result: tranquility, peace of mind.

At this point, one may wish to object: we have good reason for preferring the Epicurean view of the cosmos to its rivals. It is, after all, the view that resembles most closely the world described by modern science. Ancient atomism, whether in its Democritean or Epicurean form, looks like modern atomic theory, at least down to the time when physicists discovered that atoms were not solid bits of matter, but had an internal structure. The Epicurean view that there are multiple cosmoi in the universe resembles our modern cosmological picture of multiple galaxies. One may wonder, then, why ancient atomism did not carry the day against its rivals. There are several answers to this question, I think. First, the evidence in favor of atomism was indirect, whereas the evidence in favor of the rival theories was, to some extent, direct. We can *see* the objects around us, *hear* the sounds they make, *taste*, *smell*, and *touch* them. Our senses confirm the existence of tables and chairs, flowers and trees and the like. They don't directly confirm the existence of atoms. On the cosmic level, we can see with the naked eye the sun, moon, and planets of our solar system, but we cannot confirm, without the aid of powerful telescopes, the existence of other solar systems, let alone galaxies.

Second, ancient atomism wasn't the mathematical theory modern atomism is. Neither Democritus nor Epicurus could have told you how many kinds of atoms there were and how they were arranged in families based on their properties. They had no periodic table of the elements. When John Dalton pioneered the modern atomic theory in 1805, he posited precise mathematical relationships among the gases he had studied. Democritus had nothing like that in his favor. He had only a general idea of an indefinite number of tiny bodies of various shapes and sizes that combined in ways he could not specify. In this respect, Plato's cosmology was much more economical than that of the atomists. Granted, in one respect, the Platonic theory is definitely *not* economical: in its postulation of a world of Forms. But, in another,

Plato's theory is quite economical: the ancient atomists required a large number, perhaps an infinite number, of different kinds of atoms, while Plato built his universe out of just two triangles. The same might be said of Aristotle, who built everything from four elements and the Stoics, who built everything from two.

Third, the ancient audience would have accepted the teleological character of the cosmos much more readily than we do today. The divorce between scientific and teleological explanation is a modern creation, dating back perhaps four hundred years. Think for a moment of the teleological biology of Aristotle, which was by far the most detailed explanation of biological phenomena in the ancient world, and which was recognized by everyone as scientific. Not until the latter part of the nineteenth century did Charles Darwin offer a theory of the evolution of biological species in which teleological explanation was replaced by explanation in terms of natural selection. Today, thanks to Darwin, we would be instantly suspicious of any theory that attempted to explain the evolution of species using teleological concepts. Such a theory would probably be labeled a theory of "intelligent design" and treated as a religious, rather than a scientific theory. The same holds for cosmology. The idea that the motion of the heavenly bodies could have been explained teleologically would have seemed natural to an ancient audience, but it gradually came to be seen as unacceptable. Even after that happened, cosmologists retained God in cosmology to explain otherwise inexplicable features of the motion of the heavenly bodies. Only in the nineteenth century could the French astronomer LaPlace present a cosmological theory that did not make use of God. So, until quite recent times, science was much more friendly to teleology and the hypothesis of a divine cause than it is today.

Today, scientific cosmology traces the origin of the cosmos to the "Big Bang," which occurred almost fourteen billion years ago. Scientists can explain events in our universe by tracing them back to that initial moment. Only the moment itself is unexplained.

The question "What caused the Big Bang?" is regarded as a philosophical or theological question, rather than a scientific one. For the most part, however, cosmology has become a scientific rather than a philosophical enterprise. Scientists have reasons, based on experimental data, to decide in favor of an account of nature that does not require the use of teleology or God. This information was simply not available to an ancient audience. The result is that a theory such as Epicurus' would have seemed much less plausible to an ancient audience than it would to a modern one. The questions raised by the rival cosmologies discussed in this chapter were undecidable on the basis of anything that could have been known in antiquity. Which brings us, in the end, back to Socrates. According to Plato, Socrates did not concern himself with cosmological questions, though he did concern himself with theological ones. According to Xenophon, he was surprised that the proponents of various theories of the origin and nature of the universe could not see that the answers to the questions they raised could not be known. The debate between cosmologies that are teleological and theistic and those that are not continues today, but now it is a debate between science and religion; and that debate does not look like it is about to end any time soon.

# Translations

In the course of this book, I quote from several ancient sources, using particular modern translations. I list below the translations I use.

Presocratic Philosophers: Kirk, G. S., Raven, J. E., and Schofield, M., *The Presocratic Philosophers*, Second Edition (Cambridge: Cambridge University Press, 1983).

Protagoras: Guthrie, W. K. C., *The Sophists* (Cambridge: Cambridge University Press, 1971).

Plato: Cooper, J., ed., *Plato: Complete Works* (Indianapolis and Cambridge: Hackett Publishing Company, Inc., 1997).

Xenophon: *Conversations of Socrates*: Tredennick, H. and Waterfield, R., trans. (London: Penguin Books, 1990).

Aristotle, *Nicomachean Ethics*: Ostwald, M., trans. (Indianapolis: Bobbs-Merrill Educational Publishing, 1962).

Other quotations from Aristotle come from:

Barnes, J., ed., *The Complete Works of Aristotle*, 2 vols. (Princeton: Princeton University Press, 1984).

Hellenistic Philosophy: Long, A. A. and Sedley, D. N., eds., *The Hellenistic Philosophers*, vol. 1 (Cambridge: Cambridge University Press, 1987).

I make occasional modifications, where noted.

# Further reading

In this guide to further reading, I make no attempt to survey the entire field of ancient philosophy. Instead, I offer suggestions as to what someone who has read this book might read as the very next step in becoming acquainted with the subject. I divide the list of recommendations into two parts: primary sources and secondary sources.

## Primary sources

In addition to the translations already mentioned, I recommend the following:

### I. General surveys
### A. Organized topically:

Annas, J., ed., *Voices of Ancient Philosophy* (Oxford: Oxford University Press, 2001).

Irwin, T., ed. *Classical Philosophy* (Oxford: Oxford University Press, 1999).

### B. Organized chronologically:

Allen, R. E., ed., *Greek Philosophy: Thales to Aristotle*, third edition (New York: the Free Press, 1991).

Baird, F. E., ed., *Philosophic Classics, Volume I: Ancient Philosophy*, sixth edition (Pearson Higher Education, 2010).

Cohen, S. M., Curd, P., and Reeve, C. D. C., eds., *Readings in Ancient Greek Philosophy: from Thales to Aristotle*, fourth edition (Indianapolis: Hackett Publishing Company, Inc., 2011).

Inwood, B. and Gerson, L., eds., *Hellenistic Philosophy: Introductory Readings*, second edition (Indianapolis: Hackett Publishing Company, Inc., 1998).

Reeve, C. D. C. and Miller, P. L., eds., *Introductory Readings in Ancient Greek and Roman Philosophy* (Indianapolis: Hackett Publishing Company, Inc., 2006).

Saunders, J., ed., *Greek and Roman Philosophy after Aristotle* (New York: the Free Press, 1997).

## II. Works on individual authors and schools of philosophy

### A. Presocratic philosophy:

Many collections are available. Here is just a sample:

Barnes, J., ed., *Early Greek Philosophy* (London: Penguin Books, 1987).

Curd, P., ed., *A Presocratics Reader*, second edition (Indianapolis: Hackett Publishing Company, Inc., 2011).

Freeman, K., trans., *Ancilla to the Pre-Socratic Philosophers* (Cambridge, MA: Harvard University Press, 1983).

Graham, D. W., *The Texts of Early Greek Philosophy: The Complete Fragments and Selected Testimonies of the Major Presocratics* (Cambridge: Cambridge University Press, 2010).

McKirahan, R. D., *Philosophy Before Socrates*, second edition (Indianapolis: Hackett Publishing Company, Inc., 2011).

Waterfield, R., *The First Philosophers: the Presocratics and the Sophists* (Oxford: Oxford University Press, 2000).

### B. Plato:

Hamilton, E. and Cairns, H., eds., *The Collected Dialogues of Plato* (Princeton: Princeton University Press, 1961). An older work than Cooper, see page 173, less comprehensive but still useful.

Jowett, B., *The Dialogues of Plato*. A classic translation from the nineteenth century, now available in electronic format.

There are numerous collections of selected Platonic dialogues, as well as numerous translations of individual dialogues.

## C. Aristotle:

Ackrill, J. L., ed., *A New Aristotle Reader* (Princeton: Princeton University Press, 1987).

Irwin, T. and Fine, G., eds., *Aristotle: Selections* (Indianapolis: Hackett Publishing Company, Inc., 1996).

McKeon, R., ed., *The Basic Works of Aristotle* (New York, Random House, Inc., 1941; paper edition, 2011).

Ross, W. D., ed., *The Complete Works of Aristotle Translated into English*, 12 v. (Oxford: Oxford University Press, 1908–54). The original "Oxford Translation," now in electronic format.

## D. Cicero:

Philosophical dialogues, including *Academica*, *On Duties*, *On Fate*, *Laelius* or *On Friendship*, *Laws*, *On the Nature of the Gods*, *Tusculan Disputations*, *On Moral Ends*, *On Old Age*, *Republic*. Loeb Classical Library. (Cambridge, MA: Harvard University Press, various dates.) More recent translations of several of these works exist. I would recommend in particular Woolf, R., trans., *On Moral Ends* (Cambridge: Cambridge University Press, 2001).

## E. Epicurus and Epicureanism:

Inwood, B. and Gerson, L., eds., *The Epicurus Reader* (Indianapolis and Cambridge: Hackett Publishing Company, Inc., 1994).

Lucretius, *On the Nature of Things* (available in several modern translations).

## F. Stoicism:

### i. Seneca:

Campbell, R., trans., *Letters from a Stoic* (London: Penguin Books, 1969).

Davie, J., trans., *Dialogues and Essays* (Oxford: Oxford University Press, 2007).

### ii. Epictetus:

White, N. P., trans., *The Handbook of Epictetus* (Indianapolis: Hackett Publishing Company, Inc., 1983).

*Discourses.* Several recent translations exist, often bound with the
*Handbook.*

### iii. Marcus Aurelius:

*Meditations.* Again, several recent translations exist.

### G. Skepticism:

### i. Sextus Empiricus:

Annas, J. and Barnes, J., eds., *Outlines of Skepticism* (Cambridge:
Cambridge University Press, 2000).

Hallie, P., ed., *Selections from the Major Writings on Scepticism, Man &
God* (Indianapolis: Hackett Publishing Company, Inc., 1985).

### ii. Augustine:

King, P., trans., *Against the Academicians* and *The Teacher* (Indianapolis: Hackett Publishing Company, Inc., 1995).

## Secondary sources

As with the primary sources, I can mention only a few of the most
prominent items, and only those intended for a non-specialist
audience.

### I. Histories of Ancient Philosophy (a selection)

Adamson, P., *Classical Philosophy: A history of philosophy without
any gaps, Volume I* and *Philosophy in the Hellenistic and Roman
Worlds: A History of Philosophy without any gaps, Volume 2*
(Oxford: Oxford University Press, 2014 and 2015).

Blackson, T., *Ancient Greek Philosophy: From the Presocratics to the
Hellenistic Philosophers* (Malden, MA: Wiley–Blackwell, 2011).

Irwin, T., *Classical Thought* (Oxford: Oxford University Press,
1989).

Kenny, A., *Ancient Philosophy: A New History of Western Philosophy,
Volume I* (Oxford: Oxford University Press, 2007).

Roochnik, D., *Retrieving the Ancients: An Introduction to Greek
Philosophy* (Malden, MA: Wiley–Blackwell, 2004).

Shields, C., *Ancient Philosophy: A Contemporary Introduction*, second ed. (New York: Routledge, 2011).

**II. Series:**

Oxford University Press: *A Very Short Introduction*. Titles relevant to ancient philosophy include: Annas, J., *Ancient Philosophy* (2000) and *Plato* (2003); Barnes, J., *Aristotle* (2001); Osborne, C., *Presocratic Philosophy* (2004); and Taylor, C. C. W., *Socrates* (2000).

The University of California Press: *Ancient Philosophies*. Titles include Mason, A., *Plato* (2010); O'Keefe, T., *Epicureanism* (2010); Sellars, J., *Stoicism* (2014); and Thorsrud, H., *Ancient Skepticism* (2014).

**III. Outside the Box:**

Goldstein, R., *Plato at the Googleplex: Why Philosophy Won't Go Away* (New York: Pantheon Books, 2014).

Hadot, P., *Philosophy as a Way of Life* (Oxford: Blackwell Publishers Ltd., 1995).

Leroi, A. M., *The Lagoon: How Aristotle invented Science* (New York: Viking Penguin, 2014).

Romm, J., *Dying Every Day: Seneca at the Court of Nero* (New York: Alfred A. Knopf, 2014).

# Index